Start & Run a Home-Based Food Business

Mimi Shotland Fix

Self-Counsel Press
(a division of)
International Self-Counsel Press Ltd.
USA   Canada

Self-Counsel Press acknowledges the financial support of the Government of Canada through the Canada Book Fund (CBF) for our publishing activities.

Printed in Canada.

First edition: 2009; Reprinted: 2011, 2012

Library and Archives Canada Cataloguing in Publication

Shotland Fix, Mimi

    Start & run a home-based specialty food business / Mimi Shotland Fix.

ISBN 978-1-55180-833-8

    1. Food industry and trade — Management. 2. Home-based business — Management. 3. New business enterprises — Management. I. Title. II. Title: Start and run a home-based specialty food business.

HD62.38.S56 2009   664   C2009-900228-0

Self-Counsel Press
(a division of)
International Self-Counsel Press Ltd.

Bellingham, WA   North Vancouver, BC
USA   Canada

Contents

Notice   xiii

Acknowledgments   xv

Introduction   xvii

1 Location and Space   3

1. Start Your Business in Your Kitchen   3

    1.1   Storage and work space in your home   3

2. Finding a Kitchen Outside Your Home   4

    2.1   Kitchen incubators and shared kitchens   5

    2.2   Places that accommodate large gatherings   5

    2.3   Renting a commercial space   5

3. Get the Rental Agreement in Writing   6

2 Finding Your Product Niche   11

1. Foods Made without Heat   11

2. Stovetop, Hot Plate, and Microwave Foods   12

3. Baked Foods   12

4. Specialized Niches   12

    4.1   Convenience foods and meal parts   13

    4.2   Ethnic foods   13

    4.3   Health-oriented, allergy specific, and other special diets   13

	4.4	The seasons	13
	4.5	Fashionable foods	14
	4.6	Gift packages	14
5.		The "New" Catering	14
6.		Things to Consider before You Decide on a Product Niche	16
	6.1	Foods that are labor intensive	16
	6.2	Consider the shelf life	16
	6.3	Copyright issues on character cake pans	16
	6.4	Limit your products in the beginning	17
7.		Create a Signature Product	17
	7.1	Develop a few specialties	17
8.		Researching the Market	18

3 Preparing a Business Plan — 21

1.	Executive Summary	22
2.	Statement of Purpose	22
3.	History and Background	22
4.	Description of the Business and Products	22
5.	Company Values	22
6.	Operations and Employees	23
7.	Market Research	23
8.	Promotional Strategies	23
9.	Financing and Start-up Expenses	23
10.	Projections and Forecasts	24
11.	Personal Business Plan	24
12.	Business Planning Help	24

4 Making Your Business Legal — 29

1.		Your Business Structure	29
	1.1	Sole proprietorship	30
	1.2	Partnership	30
2.		Choose a Business Name	31
	2.1	Register your business name	31
3.		Employer Identification Number or Business Number	31
4.		Business License and Seller's Permit	32

	5.	Food Production License	32
		5.1 Food production license and legal issues	32
	6.	Insurance	33
	7.	Zoning Laws	34

5 Financial Management 37

	1.	Start-up Capital	37
		1.1 Minimalist approach	37
		1.2 Moderate approach	38
		1.3 Flush-with-capital approach	39
	2.	Bookkeeping: Keep Track of Your Business	40
		2.1 Business expenses and deductions	40
		2.2 Business income	43
		2.3 Separating business finances from personal finances	46
	3.	Hiring a Professional to Help with the Bookkeeping	46
	4.	Paying Yourself	46
		4.1 Retirement savings	47
	5.	Setting up Your Home Office	47

6 Purchasing Cooking Equipment, Utensils, and Supplies 51

	1.	Cooking Equipment	51
		1.1 Worktable and counter space	52
		1.2 Refrigerator	52
		1.3 Freezers	52
		1.4 Ovens	53
		1.5 Stovetop cooking or frying equipment	53
		1.6 Sinks	53
		1.7 Cooling rack	54
		1.8 Proof box	54
		1.9 Microwave	54
		1.10 Mixers	54
		1.11 Food processor	54
		1.12 Bread machine	54
	2.	Cooking Utensils and Other Kitchen Necessities	55
		2.1 Saucepans and stockpots	55

	2.2	Baking sheets, trays, and pans	55
	2.3	Rolling pins	55
	2.4	Measuring utensils	56
	2.5	Timers	56
	2.6	Miscellaneous small hand tools	56
	2.7	Aprons and towels	56
	2.8	Pan holders and pot holders	56
	2.9	Ingredient scale	57
	2.10	Certified scale	57
	2.11	Ingredient bins and tubs	57
	2.12	Shelving and racks	57
	2.13	Cleaning tools and supplies	57
3.	Purchasing Supplies		57
	3.1	Food supplies	58
	3.2	Holiday supplies	58
	3.3	Packaging supplies	59

7 How to Name, Package, and Label Your Products

			63
1.	Product Names		63
2.	Packaging		63
	2.1	The basics of packaging	64
	2.2	Trays and platters	65
	2.3	Gift packaging, bags, and baskets	65
	2.4	Outer packaging and transporting	65
	2.5	Shipping	65
	2.6	Eco-friendly	66
3.	Labeling Your Products		66
	3.1	Ingredient list	67
	3.2	Nutrition facts label	68
	3.3	Health claims	68
	3.4	Universal Product Code (UPC)	69

8 Pricing Products

		73
1.	Calculating the Costs	73
2.	Adjusting for Change in Cost of Goods	76

3.	Wholesale, Retail, and Courtesy Discount Prices		76
4.	Wedding Cakes and Other Exceptions to the Rule		77
	4.1	Contracts for wedding cakes and other special orders	78

9 Where to Find Your Customers — 83

1.	Wholesale: Finding Businesses that Will Sell Your Products		83
	1.1	Restaurants, diners, delis, and coffee shops	85
	1.2	Stores and markets	85
	1.3	Caterers and party planners	86
	1.4	Online merchants and catalogs	86
	1.5	Florists, gift shops, and specialty boutiques	86
2.	Retail: Finding Your Customers		86
	2.1	Street fairs and markets	86
	2.2	Mobile carts	89
	2.3	Office delivery route	89
	2.4	Wedding cakes and other specialty products	92
	2.5	Residential neighborhood sales	92
	2.6	Kitchen sales	93
	2.7	Mail order	93
	2.8	Holiday sales	93
	2.9	Celebrating year-round	95
	2.10	The custom gift business	95

10 Promoting Your Products — 101

1.	Create a Logo		101
2.	Advertising		101
3.	Marketing		102
4.	Publicity		102
	4.1	Press releases	102
5.	Public Relations		103
	5.1	Brochures	103
	5.2	Flyers	103
	5.3	Business cards	103
	5.4	Websites	106
	5.5	Portfolio	106

	5.6 Coupons	106
	5.7 Write your own ads	106
	5.8 Point-of-purchase promotional materials	106
	5.9 Promotional products	107
	5.10 Newsletters	107

11 Using and Measuring Ingredients — 111

1.	Availability and Substitutions	111
2.	Use Natural Ingredients to Extend Shelf Life	112
3.	Use Fresh Ingredients	112
4.	Find a Multifunctional Recipe	112
5.	Increasing the Ingredients	113
6.	Formatting Recipes	113
7.	Tweaking a Recipe	114
8.	Testing Product Shelf Life	114
	8.1 Freezing your products or ingredients	115
9.	Measuring Ingredients	115
10.	Utilizing the Leftovers and Excess Products	116
11.	Ingredient Equivalencies	117

12 Recipe Advice and Tips — 125

1.	Ongoing Problem Recipes or Products	125
	1.1 Occasionally good recipes go bad	126
2.	General Tips for Recipes	126
3.	Muffins and Quick Breads	128
4.	Cookies	129
5.	Bars and Brownies	130
6.	Coffee, Bundt, and Pound Cakes	131
7.	Other Cakes	131
8.	Cake Frostings	132
9.	Pies, Pastries, and Sweet Crusts	133
10.	Breads, Buns, and Breakfast Pastries	133
11.	Fruit Sweetened, No-Sugar Added Products	134

13 Production and Business Tips   139

1. Production Tips   139

    1.1 Seasonal production   139

    1.2 Scheduling production   140

    1.3 Assembly line method   140

    1.4 Being organized   141

2. Food Safety Tips   141

3. Kitchen Safety Tips   142

4. Business Tips   142

    4.1 Look professional   143

    4.2 Your food should look professional too   143

    4.3 Organize your home office   143

    4.4 Be timely   143

    4.5 Be consistent   143

    4.6 Be a thinker   144

    4.7 Problem solve   144

    4.8 Know your competition   144

    4.9 Donations   145

    4.10 Don't give away recipes   145

5. Customer Service Tips   145

    5.1 Put on a happy face   145

    5.2 Keep in contact   146

    5.3 Dealing with pushy people   146

    5.4 Observing your customers   146

    5.5 Hire good employees   146

6. Taking Care of Yourself   147

    6.1 Prioritize to reduce stress   147

    6.2 Manage your time   147

    6.3 Avoid isolation   148

    6.4 Occupational hazards   148

14 Expanding Your Business   151

1. Keeping Your Business at Home   151

    1.1 Increase production capability   152

	1.2	Upgrade equipment	152
	1.3	Renovation	152
	1.4	Increase your outlets	152
	1.5	Extend your product varieties	152
	1.6	Profit from emerging trends	152
	1.7	Continue to advertise	152
	2.	Opening a Retail Shop	153
	3.	Wholesale Space	154
	4.	Co-Packers	155
	5.	Making Decisions	155

Recipes

1	Basic Buttermilk Muffin Batter	1
2	Pumpkin Loaf	9
3	Apple Crumb Cake	19
4	Sour Cream Coffee Cake	27
5	Almond Chocolate Chip Cookies	35
6	Bakery Sugar Cookies	49
7	Gingerbread Cookies	61
8	Cappuccino Blondies	71
9	Chocolate Overdose Brownies	81
10	Chocolate Cake	99
11	Red Velvet Cake	109
12	Poppy Seed Cake	123
13	Harvest Cake Muffins	137
14	Grand Marnier Fruitcake	149

Table

| 1 | Ingredient Equivalencies | 117 |

Samples

| 1 | Sublet Agreement | 8 |
| 2 | Simplified Business Plan | 26 |

3   Repayment Contract   38

4   Investor Coupon   39

5   Monthly Expense Ledger   42

6   Monthly Income Record   45

7   Product Label   67

8   Ingredient Label   68

9   Ingredient Cost Caculator   74

10 Recipe Cost Calculator   75

11 Wedding Cake Contract   79

12 Retail Market Venue Supply Checklist   90

13 Office Delivery Route Flyer   91

14 Neighborhood Flyer   94

15 Holiday Flyer   96

16 Holiday Letter   97

17 Press Release   104

18 Retail Flycr   105

19 Recipe Format   115

Notice to Readers

Acknowledgments

I was happy being a faux pastry chef and never intended to be a writer, but sometimes things don't work out the way we plan. Thank you Professor Zencey for the encouragement to make writing a second career after the first one took an unexpected turn. The next book really will be the one we worked on.

Thanks to my publisher for making this transition possible. Editors Eileen and Tanya reshaped the manuscript so that you, my reader, would have a better understanding of running a home-based food business.

To my husband Dave, who washed all the dishes, spent hours alone, and never (hah!) complained. For my daughter Gemmae, who as a two-year old fell into a bucket of blackstrap molasses and taught me the value of safety rules. To son-in-law Eric, my always cheerful webmaster, who gladly accepted oatmeal cookies as payment. To David Jr. for the dessert table photos. Thank you to all of my family and friends for their sacrifice in eating countless test batches of baked goods. Finally, to my readers: I hope this book takes you one step closer to that first (or second!) career you always planned.

Introduction

Having a home-based food business is perfect if you're a stay-at-home parent, unemployed, or retired. It's also great for people who work outside the home and are looking for a second job to make extra money. It's especially helpful for people who are not satisfied in their present job or career, because it can be a way to ease into the food business without leaving the security of a job. If you do have a full-time job and depend on that income, don't quit yet. Give this a try and see how you like it.

For many people, the idea of owning a food business is a fantasy that seems unattainable. But with a few simple steps and very little expense, anyone can start a home-based food business and make money. The important thing is to find a product that people want (maybe you make your family's secret salsa recipe or give away jams that taste better than those you can find at the market). Once you've found the product people want, simply make it, wrap it, and deliver it.

If you have thought about a home-based food business and find it appealing but are not skilled in the kitchen, an option is to first learn the craft. Work in a food production environment (e.g., bakery, catering business, or restaurant) and you'll pick up a few skills while seeing a business from the other side of the counter.

Take courses offered through adult and continuing education programs or look for cooking schools that have an affordable certificate curriculum. Stores that sell cake and bakery supplies, especially decorating supplies, might offer classes. You can also apprentice or volunteer with a local bakery or church group.

The most important thing to do is practice at home. Spend time reading cookbooks and recipes. Read cookbooks the way you would read a novel — cover to cover. Ask questions of people you know who do cook and bake. These suggestions will give you a better footing when you start your own business.

If you can navigate around the kitchen, the steps outlined in this book will move you ahead. If your real dream is to have a large food business, the steps in this book can get you started. In the Resources file included on the CD, there are links to inspiring stories about people who began in their homes and grew their ventures into substantial, full-time businesses. That's always a possibility for you, too.

I wish there had been a book like this when I began. After graduating college I began a career in social services; but a few years later I was unemployed, a soon-to-be single parent, and worried about the future. How could I make enough money to pay the rent and child care? The bleak prospect of returning to a low-paying job was depressing so I consoled myself by baking. I made huge golden loaves of honey whole wheat bread and saucer-sized triple chocolate chip cookies. I loved to bake but had no previous business or food industry experience. I thought about baking and selling from my kitchen, so I looked for help. However, I found no guides or how-to books other than a couple of catering manuals that did not address my questions.

The catering books, while interesting, were not applicable to setting up a home-based baking business. These books focused on quantity cooking in commercially equipped kitchens for off-premises service. They told me how to create menus, transport hot foods, set up bar service, and rent linens. My needs were different. I wanted to learn how to resize recipes and set up my kitchen space for efficient quantity production. I needed help in pricing, packaging, and labeling my baked items. I also wanted to know how to find customers. I was totally unprepared, but I moved ahead. I stumbled along asking questions, making mistakes, and learning as I moved forward.

For approximately two years I continued in my kitchen until I heard about a small neighborhood pizza shop that had closed. Its production area was the same size as my home kitchen! I rented the space but had no idea how to design a commercial production area or a retail store.

There are often some limitations to using your personal budget. Professional help was cost-prohibitive for me so I continued along on my own, often unsure about my decisions. I converted a shop into a bakery and continued to ask questions. While holding on to my basic approach to home baking, I learned techniques that helped speed up my production and create more professional products. Eventually my humble beginnings resulted in an all-scratch bakery and café, a free-standing building with numerous employees. I had built a successful retail and wholesale business.

I've worked 25 years in the food industry. After owning and operating a bakery business for 15 years, I worked in other commercial kitchens as a baker and (faux) pastry chef. I also worked in the corporate food world of research and development, both as a baker/chef developing new products and creating prototypes for a national snack food company, and as a home economist, developing and testing a new generation of ovens to compete in the rapid cook arena. However, after a particularly strenuous pastry chef position, I was unable to continue the heavy physical demands of commercial baking. I returned to school but also refocused my love of baking by creating new recipes for smaller-scale baking in my home kitchen.

Early in my career, as I learned the professional approach to baking for efficient quantity production, I was able to successfully adapt many home techniques to the commercial production process. Now, after returning to my home kitchen, I've discovered that many commercial techniques can also be adapted for home use. In this book I have many shortcuts to share, because I've combined commercial and home-baking processes to give you the best of both baking worlds.

I've watched as the food industry has grown and changed into a global marketplace. I've seen that there's always a market for local homemade goods. You only have to look at the marketing techniques used by large corporations. Their labels give the impression of fresh-from-the-farm homemade goodness. Their labels literally read: *homemade*, *fresh from the oven*, and *just like grandma's*. Spend some time in the grocery store, convenience mart, or anywhere food is displayed (don't forget vending machines). Take a stroll through the green markets and look at what people are buying and eating. Look around at your local hometown eateries, neighborhood shops, farmers' markets, and countryside stands. What do you see? *Homemade goodness rules!*

Throughout the book I will provide you with many suggestions for your home-based food business. This book is written for all levels of bakers and people with a wide variety of business goals. Read through the whole book, even the parts that do not seem to apply to your situation, because there are valuable tips in each area and suggestions that may help you improve your skill set. If you are already skilled at one of the steps, then good for you! If you already have a great recipe (or ten!), you're way ahead, but there are other steps involved. For those of you currently in business who want answers to specific questions, or simply want to grow your business, this book will help you too. Please remember that you're not alone. My website (www.BakingFix.com) continues to help support your efforts. Visit me there, ask questions, and learn about other owners of home-based food businesses.

You can experiment and go slow, or charge forward. By starting in your kitchen with no pressure of expensive overhead, you have the ability to go as fast or as slow as you would like. If you want to have a food business but cannot do it from your own kitchen, this book will give you alternative ideas.

This book includes everything you must know about starting and staying in business. With detailed, step-by-step advice, this practical guide supplies you with all of the key ingredients to transform your dream into reality. Food products will always be in demand so there will always be a business waiting for you.

Good luck and enjoy — the best to all of you!

— Mimi

Basic Buttermilk Muffin Batter

Prepare the additions and set aside.

Preheat oven to 375°F and line the muffin pan with paper cups or use pan spray.

In a medium bowl, beat together the egg, oil, sugar, buttermilk, and vanilla. In a separate bowl, stir together the flour, baking powder, baking soda, and salt.

Pour the dry ingredients on top of the wet and stir gently until mixed. Some small lumps are okay. Then stir in the prepared fruit or other additions. This should be a thick batter.

Divide batter into 12 medium or 6 large muffins, filling the pans almost to the top.

Bake for 20 to 30 minutes depending on size. Turn down the oven heat if the tops are getting too brown. They will be done when a finger pressed gently on top leaves no imprint.

Cool thoroughly before wrapping and storing. These keep for two days; can be frozen for up to six months.

For variations of this recipe see the file on the CD:

Muffins and Quick Breads

Yield: Makes 6 large or 12 medium muffins

1-2 cups total additions (dried or seasonal fruit, chopped; nuts or coconut)

1 large egg

$1/3$ cup oil

$1/2$ teaspoon baking soda

$1/3$ cup granulated sugar

1 cup buttermilk
(or $7/8$ cup milk with 2 tablespoons vinegar or lemon juice)

2 teaspoons vanilla

$2 1/2$ cups all-purpose unbleached flour

2 teaspoons baking powder

$1/2$ teaspoon salt

Chapter 1
Location and Space

The first step in starting a home-based food business is deciding whether your kitchen is up to the task. You may already be aware that you need to find a bigger kitchen to do your work. This chapter will help you decide what will work best for you and how to utilize the space you have.

1. Start Your Business in Your Kitchen

Most home kitchens have the basics — hot and cold running water, a decent floor with solid walls — which can be used for home-based food production. Even a tiny apartment-sized kitchen can work well enough to get you started. (See section **1.1** for how to work in a small space.) If you don't have a good working stove or refrigerator, it's still possible to start a business with a product that needs no appliances. Chapter 2 has suggestions to get you started.

I strongly suggest that if you have no food service background but are interested in starting this enterprise, start by using your existing kitchen. Don't remodel until you are sure that starting a home-based food business is what you want to do.

It's wonderful to have the ability to earn income just by using your kitchen. Just make sure that you, or anyone else using the kitchen, understand that business foods must be handled differently than personal foods. For example, dipping a finger into the chocolate filling may be tempting, but spreading germs and bacteria can adversely affect your customers. One sick customer can make you a target for the health department and put you out of business.

1.1 Storage and work space in your home

If you have a lot of storage space in your home, your biggest problem may be organization. Designate and label certain areas or shelves as "Business." Everything should be dated and labeled with contents.

Let anyone using the kitchen know your rules — this includes guests who might wander in while you're not around and help themselves to the rolls and salad you've just prepared for the next day's delivery.

If you don't have enough storage, look around your home for creative ways to turn unused space into business space. Your health inspector visits many other home-based food businesses, and might have suggestions for unusual storage ideas he or she has observed.

Nonfood items such as packaging materials can be stored anywhere. Perhaps the dining room can hold a cabinet or shelves; use the top shelf in a linen closet; or keep a few things on a shelf under your table. Food that's been opened needs to stay in the kitchen, pantry, or dining room, but unopened bags and boxes of ingredients can be left in their original containers and stored elsewhere. Be careful that you don't forget what you have and buy too much; an inventory list can be helpful but you must remember to keep it updated or it won't be of any help.

It is also important that you do not store food near moisture or in unsanitary surroundings, even if the packages are sealed. I walked into a friend's bathroom and saw five bags of sugar in her bathtub. She said there'd never been a problem but the potential is there. Note that a health inspector would not approve of this situation, so it's not a good idea to store food products in the bathroom.

Never store food directly on the floor; it's unsanitary and a health code violation in every locality I'm aware of. Check with your health inspector to see how many inches of clearance above the floor is needed and make or buy small pallets on which to stack your goods. Then you can easily clean under the pallets with a broom or vacuum without having to move everything. Garden centers and discount stores have plant trolleys that can be used as pallets. They roll, can hold a lot of weight, and work well for small spaces.

Preferably, keep all your small baking equipment (e.g., measuring cups, spoons, spatulas) in a central basket or tub. Do the same with the small cans, jars, and boxes of ingredients such as salt, baking powder, baking soda, and extracts. When you're ready to work, all you do is take out the tub or basket of tools and the container for equipment.

Having lots of work and storage space is ideal but if you have only a small place, you must be creative. Think about the kinds of foods you can produce that take up less production space. If counter and table space is tight, get a folding table or two. If the refrigerator is small, stay away from recipes requiring refrigeration of ingredients, or substitute shelf-stable ingredients. Instead of whole milk, use the less expensive powdered milk; buttermilk also comes in powdered form; or use water, coffee, juices, or teas. Limit your product line to items that use the same basic ingredients to save space. See Chapter 11, section **4.**, for more information about multifunctional recipes.

2. Finding a Kitchen Outside Your Home

You can still have a home-based food business even if you must use another location for production. Your home can be used as the business base, from where you conduct your business, keep your books, and correspond with clients and suppliers. If you find the laws regulating homemade food production in your locality prohibit you from pursuing work in your own kitchen, there are some ways to deal with your particular problems without having the expense of renovation or renting a retail storefront. (For more information on laws and zoning, see Chapter 4.)

When you are looking for a work space outside your home, you will need to consider what the place offers you. Each facility will be set up differently; the place you decide on should have the basic equipment and work space sufficient for your needs.

If you are going to leave any supplies at the site, it's advisable to have a locked storage area to prevent both theft and contamination. If you cannot safely store your items there, you will need to transport these items each time you go to the production site. Don't rely on your memory. Make a master list of all your supplies and check everything off before you go, and again when you leave the site.

The following sections discuss options for the use of a kitchen outside your home.

2.1 Kitchen incubators and shared kitchens

Small food businesses are a growing trend. To accommodate these entrepreneurial start-ups, a relatively new business model is developing. Centers known by various names — small business development centers, food innovation centers, kitchen incubators, food ventures, or shared kitchens — are being created to help support new (or young and growing) food businesses. These places are licensed facilities and are equipped for commercial production. Most of these centers also offer business guidance.

Each facility is different and has its own rules and prerequisites. Some expect you to have a business certificate before signing up; some offer a complete package of business and production help; and some let users sign up for only the services they need. These facilities used to be found only in large cities or were associated with universities or nonprofit organizations. But new ones continue to open, and many are now private, for-profit businesses.

In the Resources file on the CD you will find a list of such facilities in the US and in Canada. You can also do an Internet search for any new facilities which continue to open.

For entrepreneurs without the expertise or money to invest in a full-scale business, using an incubator kitchen is a wonderful way to start, especially since many of these centers offer basic business and production help. It can be just the support you need to be successful.

If using an incubator kitchen interests you, be aware that it will involve fees. While this is less expensive than renting a storefront, you will need some capital to go this route.

If you are kitchen savvy (perhaps you've already worked in commercial food service or have a culinary degree), there might be a facility near you where you can rent just the space, without paying for their other services.

2.2 Places that accommodate large gatherings

Another possibility is to use the kitchen facilities in a town hall, community center, house of worship, or other places which often have large production areas to accommodate gatherings. These places might welcome additional revenue. If these kitchens are not already certified, it might be easily done. A formal written agreement between you and the facility is recommended. This is further explained in section **3**.

2.3 Renting a commercial space

You can sometimes work out an agreement with a business owner who already operates in a licensed kitchen. There are restaurants, catering companies, delis, coffee shops, bakeries, markets, and natural foods stores that are closed during certain hours — they might welcome the extra income from renting their space to you while their business is not operating. If you are producing a small quantity of products and only need a kitchen one day a week, many food businesses may welcome you on days when they are closed.

You could also look into renting space from a small restaurant during its off hours. The clean-up crew for the restaurant might be finished before midnight and the first shift might not start lunch until ten in the morning. Perhaps there's a small cake business in your town that only uses their kitchen three or four days a week and would love to make some extra money by renting it out to you when they're not using it. These places might also barter space so that you can pay for the kitchen with your fresh-made items or your time.

It's important that the commercial space is licensed and has the equipment you need to process your products. The basics should be in good working order and up to code — refrigeration, sinks, electric and plumbing, walls, and floors.

How is the kitchen equipped? Does it fit your needs? Not all commercial kitchens are alike. Perhaps you need a stovetop with two burners, but the facility only has a convection oven. Make a list of your needs, such as counter space, mixer, food processor, oven capacity, cooling rack, and baking pans. Can you supply and transport any equipment that the facility lacks? Ideally the place will have secured space where you can lock up your ingredients and small equipment. Otherwise, be prepared to haul all your materials with you.

Also consider your personal safety when choosing a place. You may be in a different, unfamiliar location. Your work hours may be during off hours when it will be dark outside.

Is the surrounding neighborhood safe? These considerations should factor into your decision on whether or not to use a particular kitchen.

You should also get sign a formal written agreement, as explained in the next section.

3. Get the Rental Agreement in Writing

It is very important to have a signed agreement that is specific to your needs and the needs of the owner of the subletting business. (See Sample 1 for more information about what to cover in your sublet agreement.) Your business depends on your ability to use the facility for production. A lease agreement will protect both parties.

If the owner objects to a formal agreement, mention that an agreement protects him or her as well as you. I would be very suspicious of anyone who refuses this request. Anyone who objects to a written agreement usually isn't a good choice for business dealings.

Occasionally an informal agreement works, but it basically relies more on honor of fulfillment rather than an enforceable written contract. Issues often arise with an informed agreement and bad feelings can happen, especially when money is involved.

A written agreement can help clear up any misunderstandings that might occur. It doesn't need to be anything fancy, just a list of agreed terms. Even if you're bartering for the space (e.g., you pay the owner or business in cakes and cookies), it's best to have a written agreement because it protects everyone. Don't forget to make two copies, dated and signed by both parties. For added protection, be sure to have a witness to the signatures.

In your contract you will need to clearly describe the following:

- Specify times when you can use the space.

- Define what the rent is and when it will be paid (e.g., monthly, quarterly, or on a per-use basis). You may also want to include how the rent is to be paid (e.g., $50 per month plus a dozen muffins each time the space is used).

- Discuss how the utility costs will be divided (e.g., percentage of the utilities, flat monthly fee, or included in the rent).

- Licensing: The agreement should include the current license number or the name of the licensing agency for the facility.

- Detail what equipment and supplies you can use.

- Define who will be responsible for breakage or nonfunctioning equipment.

- Specify who is responsible for clean up. For example, what if the oven is filthy or the sink is clogged before you arrive?

- Discuss storage of your items. Will there be secured cabinets to avoid pilfering or contamination of your property?

- Include information about insurance coverage. Are you covered under the owner's insurance or do you need your own?

Include anything else, no matter how silly you feel about mentioning it (e.g., where to park if it's within a city district). Little things can potentially become big problems if they are not discussed in the written agreement.

Sample 1 is an example of a sublet agreement with a business owner. Included on the CD is a Sublet Worksheet that you can use if you decide to rent from a business owner.

SUBLET AGREEMENT

Use of Kitchen Facility

Date: March 23, 20--

This sublet agreement between James Owner and Martha Kitchener is for use of the kitchen located in the Rye House Annex, 49 Potato Street, Mytown.

This facility is currently licensed by Mytown Health Agency. Use of this space by Martha Kitchener includes the kitchen, related production areas, and the following equipment:

- Sinks with hot and cold running water
- Refrigeration during production time
- Two worktables and adjacent counter space
- Mixer(s)
- Ovens, range, and stovetops
- Cooling racks, proof box, sheet pans, stockpots, knives, and any miscellaneous tools in the kitchen area
- Cleaning equipment (mop, bucket, miscellaneous supplies)
- Use of one four-shelf pantry cabinet, with lock

Both parties will maintain cleanliness according to licensing agency requirements.

Days and hours covered: Sunday to Friday beginning each evening at 10:00 p.m. and ending at 4:00 a.m. the following morning. Locked storage area with 24-hour access for duration of lease. Additional production time will be negotiated separately as the need arises.

Rental amount: $50 per month, paid by the first day of each month, plus two dozen muffins for each time the facility is used. (Muffin choice is at the discretion of the baker.) Rent includes use of equipment, utilities, insurance, and repairs.

Length of contract: Will continue as long as rent is paid. Either party can end lease by providing thirty (30) days' written notice.

Signature: _____   Signature: _____
Facility owner/manager: James Owner   Tenant: Martha Kitchener
Phone: (555) 555-0000   Phone: (555) 555-5555
Address: 126 Potato Avenue, Mytown   Address: 1467 Hobart Court, Mytown

Signature: _____
Witness: _____
Phone: (555) 555-4444
Address: 1637 Rolling Pin Avenue, Mytown

Pumpkin Loaf

Preheat oven to 350°F and grease 3 medium (7 x 3) loaf pans.

In a large bowl, mix together the sugar, oil, eggs, pumpkin, and liquid.

In a 4-cup measure, lightly spoon in the flour then add the baking soda, salt, and spices. Stir, then add to the liquid ingredients and mix thoroughly. Add raisins, if using.

Spoon this thin batter into your pans and bake 35 to 50 minutes, until the tops are firm to the touch and leave no finger imprint.

Cool before wrapping. These keep for one week at room temperature, three weeks in the fridge, and six months frozen.

Also makes excellent muffins.

For variations of this recipe see the file on the CD:

Muffins and Quick Breads

Yield: 3 medium
(7 x 3) loaves

3 cups sugar

1 cup vegetable oil

4 large eggs

1 (15-16 oz) can pumpkin

$2/3$ cup water, cider, juice, or wine

$3 1/2$ cups all-purpose flour

2 teaspoons baking soda

$1 1/2$ teaspoons salt

2 teaspoons cinnamon

1 teaspoon nutmeg

$1/2$ teaspoon allspice

Optional: 1 cup raisins

Chapter 2
Finding Your Product Niche

If you currently have a specialty, or even just recipes you enjoy making — whether baking cookies, creating ethnic foods, or preserving fresh fruits — profit from what you already feel comfortable producing. If friends and relatives rave about your moist banana bread, or your decorated birthday cakes are the hit of the neighborhood, start by concentrating on those ideas to create a niche for your business.

If you like to work in your kitchen but aren't sure about a product direction, read through the following sections. For specific recipes, consult cookbooks, food magazines, and the Internet. If baking is your main interest, this book has some great recipes and the CD includes many more. The recipes included in the book and on the CD are some of my best-selling baked goods with variations to help you create your own specialty items.

The following sections include ideas for recipes, ranging in difficulty from easy to expert (some don't even need a stove) and are intended to encourage your imagination.

1. Foods Made without Heat

The following items can be made without an oven or stovetop, and several are quite simple to do:

- Bulk ingredients repackaged into consumer sizes (e.g., flours, seeds, pasta, candies)

- Bulk ingredients mixed for snacks (e.g., trail mix, party nuts, dried fruits)

- Spice and herb mixtures (e.g., vegetable or fruit salad dressing mix) — you could include recipes and menu suggestions with the mixes

- Gift baskets with fruits, candy, jams, cookies

- Homegrown or local fruits and vegetables repackaged into ready-to-use form; make fresh fruit or vegetable salads and salsas

- Trays (e.g., breakfast, deli, vegetable, dessert) or brown bag and boxed lunches using store-bought foods; repackage dinners, snacks, or meals for dieters (be sure to include calorie information)

- Dry mixes for bread, cakes, muffins, and cookies; include instructions with the mixes

- Frozen or refrigerated dough; include baking instructions

- Specialty cookies or treats such as rum balls or bourbon balls

- Specialty drinks such as smoothies, juices, and lemonades

- Frozen desserts such as ice cream, frozen yogurt, sherbet, gelato, ices, and sorbets

2. Stovetop, Hot Plate, and Microwave Foods

The following items can be prepared with the help of a small, inexpensive heating appliance:

- Candy or fudge, including nut brittles, chocolate bark, haystacks, and patties

- Dipped items such as chocolate-covered pretzels, potato chips, dried fruits, and purchased cookies (ever tasted a crème-filled chocolate sandwich cookie dipped in chocolate?)

- No-bake cookies such as Rocky Road or peanut butter balls

- Jams, jellies, preserves

- Processed (i.e., canned, frozen, refrigerated) fruits and vegetables; fruit compotes, chutneys, sauces

- Pizzelles, waffles, pancakes, or crepes made with small countertop specialty appliances such as a waffle iron, pizzelle baker, or crepe maker

- Fried items such as donuts, beignets, fritters, or funnel cakes

- Meal parts, such as salads, slaws, and other side dishes; or stovetop foods such as soups, stews, or vegetables (for more ideas on meal parts, see section **5.**)

3. Baked Foods

The following list is an overview of the extensive baked goods category. The skill level for these items ranges from easy to expert:

- Breakfast items such as muffins, coffee cakes, scones, biscuits, or sweet buns

- Granolas

- Breads such as artisan, yeast, or quick breads

- Cookies, biscotti, brownies, bars, or whoopee pies

- All-occasion cakes such as pound, bundt, layer, and sheet cakes

- Specialty cakes such as wedding, anniversary, birthday, and graduation

- Small pastries, cupcakes, and petit fours

- Fruitcakes (you'd be surprised at the market for these holiday cakes)

- Tarts, pies, and quiches (sweet or savory)

- Hors d'oeuvres and canapés

- Casseroles, vegetable dishes, entrées

- Dog treats (really, there's a market for these)

4. Specialized Niches

Another approach is to look at food in specialized areas, such as ethnic foods or foods for special diets. Specializing can help you think about food from a different perspective and perhaps come up with ideas for products not yet available in your community. If you already have an interest in one of the following areas, or something looks appealing, explore the possibilities.

4.1 Convenience foods and meal parts

Create a weeknight menu and offer delivery of hot, ready-to-eat foods. Or, instead of dealing with the concept of providing full meals, break it down into a narrow area of the meal. For example, specialize in main course casseroles or vegetable dishes. If these ideas interest you, read section **5.** in this chapter, and sections **2.5** and **2.6** in Chapter 9.

4.2 Ethnic foods

You can create ethnic foods that are specific to certain cultures that most people don't usually make themselves. There are many ethnic foods you could make such as salsa, baklava, naan, tapenade, or hummus.

4.3 Health-oriented, allergy specific, and other special diets

Health foods, a small but growing market, include foods that are whole grain, organic, natural, chemical free, trans fat free, vegan, and vegetarian, and are often related to the eat-local movement.

If you have an interest in allergy-related foods, you *must* do research and work with a dietitian who can guide your product offerings.

Other special diets include those for people who are diabetic, or those who must restrict certain foods such as salt. Here, too, you need to thoroughly research your potential products and talk to a professional dietitian.

4.4 The seasons

Take advantage of the different seasons when people like to celebrate special occasions and holidays. Keep in mind that most food products can be changed to fit different holidays. Sugar cookies can be baked using different cutters; basic cakes can have holiday-related toppers; candies can be molded into various designs. Sometimes simply using color is enough to market your regular products as holiday specialties, such as tinting your cakes and cookies green for St. Patrick's Day or tying a red ribbon around your sweet breads for Valentine's Day.

4.4a Winter

Many businesses thrive during the winter season. Homemade goods take center stage for the weeks between Thanksgiving and New Year's, when many popular products sell themselves. Seasonal breads, decorated cakes, candies, and cookie trays are a specialty. Even fruitcakes (contrary to those silly jokes) are huge sellers.

Although food products cannot be stored for long periods the way most consumer goods can be shelved, there are ways to increase your preparation time. For example, my fruitcake production begins in July. Biscotti and candies have an exceptionally long shelf life, as do dried fruits and spiced nut mixes. Making any of these products will allow you to produce more than if you had to make everything fresh during the relatively short holiday season.

Don't forget New Year's celebrations (champagne cakes), Presidents' Day (anything with cherries), and Valentine's Day (chocolate and anything heart shaped).

4.4b Spring

In spring there is St. Patrick's Day (Irish soda bread, shamrock cookies, and anything green), Easter (put together baskets with pastel-colored candy and cookies), Mother's Day and Father's Day celebrations, and graduation cakes.

4.4c Summer

Summer is the time for fresh fruit and farmers' markets; Canada Day celebrations (red and white); Fourth of July celebrations (anything red, white, and blue); and picnic or backyard barbecues where handheld foods (brownies and cookies) are great options.

4.4d Fall

Think of "harvest" for fall. Mixing together different kinds of produce in your muffins and sweet breads makes for great sellers. Add apples and pears to your products, and for Halloween, use pumpkin to flavor your baked goods.

4.5 Fashionable foods

There's always something new and trendy with foods. Look regularly at food magazines and keep an eye on the covers of consumer magazines. Watch the Food Network. Skim new cookbook titles and read newspaper food columns. Get a subscription to *Modern Baking* or a similar trade magazine, and visit Internet food sites and online bakeries. The websites for some of these are listed in the Resources section on the CD.

4.6 Gift packages

People are always looking for gifts, and food is often the choice since it's "one size fits all." Any of your food items can be placed in trays, tins, baskets, and boxes for a special look. Section **2.3** in Chapter 7 has packaging suggestions, and sections **2.8** to **2.10** in Chapter 9 have numerous ideas for marketing your gift packages.

5. The "New" Catering

The catering industry has been undergoing a change. In the past it was considered a full-service business and included menu development, event planning, extensive equipment, and numerous employees. Complete meals were prepared in a licensed kitchen facility, then transported to another location for consumption.

The concept of catering now incorporates an abbreviated form. A self-described caterer can exclude the full-service side and provide only the preparation of take-out type foods and meal parts. This is often called home meal replacement (HMR), a term used in the supermarket industry. These days, customers might say they need a caterer when they simply want someone to prepare a tray of muffins, sandwiches, or desserts.

When checking with your local health department or licensing agency, make sure you understand the terminology. Laws for the traditional catering license are often different from a license for cooking and baking, so it's up to you to understand what the difference is where you live. In my locality, the home kitchen is never acceptable for catering but can be approved for home baking, with restrictions on meat and dairy products. My inspector was very strict in that I'm not allowed to "cater" in my home kitchen, but with a baking permit I'm allowed to prepare certain meals or meal parts. For example, preparing a vegan meal or some vegetarian meals is acceptable. I'm just not allowed to use the word "cater."

With prepared foods continuing to hold a large market share, the business opportunities are extraordinary. Regardless of our economic times, offices always order food for meetings, and working adults favor dinners-to-go or meal parts. If you bake traditional breakfast fare (e.g., muffins, sweet breads, coffee cakes), you might be able to advertise breakfast catering. Items you don't make, such as Danish pastries or bagels, might be sold along with cream cheese, fruit, and juices. Hot beverages can be made on-site. If you have an ethnic specialty or make health-oriented foods that are low-calorie, allergy-free, vegetarian, or vegan, you can cater these items.

If you decide that this line of business is for you but your home kitchen cannot be licensed, read Chapter 1, section **2.**, about renting space. If a full catering business is your goal, begin here and see how you like the work. Self-Counsel Press has a book, *Start & Run a Catering Business*, that could help you start your own catering business if you decide it's right for you.

The following is a brief list of menu items, many of which you probably prepare at home for family meals. This kind of catered food does not need to be fancy. Most customers are more interested in food that tastes good (with familiar flavors) rather than cuisine that sounds exotic.

- **Canapés, crudités, hors d'oeuvres**: Most of these items are miniature versions of traditional foods. Add as many local and seasonal items as available.

- **Soups, stews, chili:** You can make seasonal vegetable stews, cold summer soups, or any number of things that need a spoon. It's best to deliver soups and stews hot, but it's not always possible to do so. If foods need reheating, use microwavable containers.

- **Salads:** There are a variety of salads you can make, including pasta salad, mixed seasonal fruit, bean, and classic green. Make sure you give customers a choice between at least two different dressings. You could also provide small rolls or biscuits to accompany each serving.

- **Sandwiches:** If you don't make bread, use bakery bread from another business.

Try to avoid factory produced sliced breads. Avoiding these reinforces the idea that you are a homemade food business. Create boxed or bag lunches for meetings and gatherings of any type.

- **Strudels and stuffed breads:** Savory fillings rolled up in pastry or bread doughs are unusual variations to the typical sandwich; they also work well as dinner entrées. The fillings can be as simple as slices of cheese and vegetables, but in this unusual form, these products seem special. The "Pies, Pastries, and Sweet Crusts" file on the CD has ideas for making such items, which can become a signature offering for your business.

- **Desserts:** In addition to any items from your product line, offer seasonal fresh fruit bowls; fruit trifles; or gooey, sticky, and messy foods not typically offered by businesses. A variety is always good to have — people like to have choice.

For all your menu items, it's your responsibility to think about what the customers need to fully enjoy your service. Envision what happens once they have your food. Do the provisions need reheating? Are serving utensils necessary? What about condiments or plates? The purpose of "catering" is to cater to the customer's basic needs and then go the extra mile. Provide a garbage bag for the customer's convenience.

Provide a handout with written instructions, details about your menu, and an expression of thanks for the business. Call the customer a few days later and ask if everything was okay. Following up with a phone call shows you go the extra mile and encourages future business.

6. Things to Consider before You Decide on a Product Niche

By now you should have a list of product possibilities. Keep these products in mind when you read through Chapter 9 about where to find customers. Every food niche has pros and cons, so it's important to select the best fit for your interests, lifestyle, and goals. Before you settle on your product line, there are some miscellaneous issues to consider which might not be obvious to those without a background in the food industry. None of the following issues are insurmountable, but they are issues you might need to address.

6.1 Foods that are labor intensive

When you look at different products and particular recipes, always think about how much work it is to create and if the potential result is worth it. For a brief time I created jelly-roll style cakes and hated making every single fussy one. At one time I briefly considered baking angel food cakes, but I hated separating yolks and whites and finding something to do with the leftover yolks. Unless you really love to work with fussy foods, think about all the implications when you read recipes.

Yeast breads are labor intensive, need a long rise and bake time, and take up a lot of space in your oven. Artisan breads made from a sourdough starter are even more time-consuming. Both kinds of breads need a dedicated approach, so if you choose foods in this category, price your products so that you'll make money.

Fine-quality chocolate needs tempering, which is a special handling process. Learn about this technique before deciding on candy, dipped items, or chocolate-covered cakes and pastries. Investigate the faux (dipping) chocolates, which are of a different quality but are easier to handle.

6.2 Consider the shelf life

Shelf life refers to how long a product can sit on the shelf and still be considered fresh. There is a public misconception about what it means to be "fresh" and "day old." Every product has its own shelf life and every recipe is different, so you'll need to do some testing.

As a general rule, long shelf-life items are granolas, biscotti, fruitcakes, most candies, and preserved or canned fruits and vegetables. Many people make long shelf-life items and stockpile their wares until the selling season arrives.

Short shelf-life items include breakfast pastries, fresh fruit pies, and recipes that state, "best eaten when warm."

6.3 Copyright issues on character cake pans

Be aware of copyright fees on licensed character cake pans.* These pans are meant for personal use only, not for selling the cakes you make with them. Even retail bakeries are under restrictions and must pay huge royalty fees for using them. Companies owning these copyrights are protective and will pursue individuals for copyright infringement.

If you are interested in selling character cakes, I suggest you create your own character design or use shaped, novelty cake pans not restricted by copyright. To know which pans are restricted, visit the Wilton website (URL included in the Resources file on the CD) and view the shaped pans section. The restricted pans will state, "For home use only."

---

*Character cake pans are pans shaped like known figures in popular culture such as Bugs Bunny, Donald Duck, etc.

6.4 Limit your products in the beginning

When you're just starting your business, it's best to limit the number of products you sell. If you have one thing that you already make very well, start by capitalizing on that. Until you have more experience, this will help you concentrate on learning the business. Especially if you're doing it part time to supplement your income, start with a small number (e.g., two or three at the most); if you're aiming for a full-scale business, try starting with fewer items and add on slowly as you get a sense of how much you can handle and what products sell better. If you produce fewer items, you will naturally limit the number of different ingredients, packaging materials, and labels you'll need.

If you want to offer variety, make a line extension. A line extension is a slight variation on what you already produce. Sugar cookies can become snickerdoodles by adding a cinnamon and sugar topping, or a plain muffin batter can yield both blueberry and chocolate chip muffins. Even plain pickles with the addition of spices can help you offer several choices. Providing choice for the customer is also a good sales tool. The customer asks, "Which one do I want?" which encourages a more positive thought process than, "Do I want this or not?"

Don't discard an idea because it seems too simple. Everyone makes impulse purchases for items that are convenient or that they don't make for themselves, such as coffee and Rice Krispies® bars.

7. Create a Signature Product

A signature product is something you make that no on else does. It can take a few years for your signature product to get recognition, but you can generate steady business with a product uniquely yours. If you already have a secret recipe, dress it up so that it looks and tastes different than everyone else's. Or look around in cookbooks and magazines, and search the Internet for ideas. The trick is to take an idea and make it your own. Even if you have always been better at copying than creating, ask for suggestions from friends, family, coworkers, and neighbors, and experiment from there.

With no competition for your product, you can charge more and encourage repeat specialty orders. Ideally, your signature product would be a must-have for certain occasions — perhaps a Pink Champagne Cake for Mother's Day, a specialty Breakfast Bread Basket for morning office meetings, or Candyland Cupcakes for baby and wedding showers.

There's a cookie business in Minneapolis that began by offering only oatmeal chocolate chip cookies. Owned by Anne and Dennis Tank, Tank Goodness delivers warm cookies in a Mini Cooper. On several levels they set themselves apart — still-warm cookies baked in a home kitchen and delivered in a cute vehicle. They have a charming website, which can be found following the link listed in the Resources section on the CD.

7.1 Develop a few specialties

Become very good at making a few things instead of average at making a wide variety. A woman I knew in Georgia had a solid business with regular customers. She made basic cakes and sweet breads, and a few cookies and brownies. As she showed me her order form, she said, "I do these things and I do them very, very well. My customers can always count on getting the same excellent cake each time they order. And I can count on them to keep ordering." Go for perfection; be better at making what you make than anyone else.

If your food quality, service, price, and convenience are better than that of other businesses, you are off to a great start. Perhaps that's all you need to make money. But business can entail more than just the basics. You don't need to resort to gimmickry to have a successful business, but creating something uniquely yours can give you a tremendous edge.

8. Researching the Market

Before you can decide on a product, you may need to do market research. Market research is a logical, objective, and thorough method of collecting data to analyze your target market. It's used to understand your competition and your business potential. In other words, you need to research what people are buying and find potential products that would be a good fit for your market.

Your market research should cover a variety of stores, farmers' markets, and online vendors. Keep a small notebook handy as you visit these places. Watch what people are buying and eating. Look at the pricing and packaging. You will need to answer the following questions:

- How much do these items cost?

- What kinds of labels are used?

- Does the packaging enhance or detract from the product?

Remember to take notes or use a recording device so you don't forget the details. Don't worry about the store manager seeing you. If a clerk asks if you need help, mumble that you need time to look for a gift. Purchase anything that looks intriguing or that you can learn from. When I do market research I always buy a product if I want to taste the flavor, understand the texture, or want to thoroughly inspect the label and package.

Do a web search and bookmark sites that have interesting or helpful information. Look through newspapers and magazines for articles and advertisements. Pick up menus, flyers, and brochures; keep them in a central place for easy reference, such as in a file folder or desk drawer. Keep copies of the information you find. Later, when you're ready to design a flyer or brochure, you'll have samples from area businesses from which to draw ideas.

Ask people for feedback when they sample your products, but be aware that the information you gather might not be truthful. Rely on your eyes and instinct, and watch people when they give you their opinions. For whatever reason, maybe it's just human nature, but people often tell you what they think you want to hear. If possible, seek individuals whose opinions you trust and who will be honest with you.

Trade magazines are another source of valuable information. These magazines are sometimes free to customers who own a business, or are about to start a business. *Baking Buyer* and *Modern Baking* keep track of trends, have great ideas, and provide supplier ads with websites and toll-free phone numbers for requesting additional information. Over the years I've found industry suppliers to be exceptionally helpful in my market research.

Having a great recipe or choosing a trendy category of food does not give you a guaranteed best-selling item. Customers can be fickle, times can change, and cupcakes can follow croissants into oblivion. Always stay current with the newest trends.

Apple Crumb Cake

Prepare apples. Place in a bowl, cover with sugar, and set aside.

Prepare streusel: In a separate bowl, mix together all of the dry streusel ingredients. Pour in the oil and water, and mix thoroughly. This should be a crumbly streusel consistency. If too moist, add flour; if too dry, sprinkle in water. Add nuts, if using. Mix and set aside.

Preheat oven to 350°F and grease or spray cake pan.

Prepare cake: In a large bowl, mix the oil, eggs, and vanilla. Add the apple mixture, including all liquid, in the bowl.

Combine the flours, baking soda, cinnamon, and salt, then mix into the wet ingredients. Add the nuts, if using. This should be a very thick batter. (At this point, batter can be refrigerated up to one week. Stir before using.)

Scoop into a greased 9 x 13 pan, spreading batter into the corners; sprinkle on the streusel. Bake for 50 to 60 minutes or longer, until the top feels firm and the cake pulls away from the sides of the pan.

Cover when cool. It's easier to cut the next day. Keeps at room temperature (except in hot weather) for one week, in the fridge for two weeks, or in the freezer for up to six months.

For variations of this recipe see the file on the CD:

Coffee, Bundt, and Pound Cakes

Cake

4 cups chopped apples with skin (approximately 4 large apples)

2 cups granulated sugar

1/2 cup oil

2 large eggs

2 teaspoons vanilla extract

2 cups whole wheat pastry flour

1 cup all-purpose flour

2 teaspoons baking soda

2 teaspoons cinnamon

1 teaspoon salt

Optional: 1 cup chopped walnuts

Streusel

This recipe makes more than you need; keep unused portion refrigerated for up to one month or frozen for up to six months. Can be used for sprinkling on other baked goods.

2 cups whole wheat pastry flour

1 cup granulated sugar

1/2 teaspoon salt

Optional: 1 teaspoon cinnamon

1/2 cup oil

3 tablespoons water

Optional: 1 cup chopped walnuts

Chapter 3
Preparing a Business Plan

A business plan is what moves your idea from a daydream to a realistic vision for the future. It will help you define your goals and outline what you need to do to achieve them. There are many facets of starting a business, so the real value in creating a business plan is that it forces you to research new, unfamiliar areas. You'll discover your strengths and weaknesses and learn about issues and details you had not previously considered. Finally, you will gain an understanding of the day-to-day reality of operating a perishable food business.

A business plan will also show others that you are serious about your ambitions. A detailed plan communicates your ideas and provides potential financiers with answers. From friends and family to potential backers and suppliers who will be extending you credit, people will respect that your business is based on a rational, thoughtful approach. If you have enough capital to invest in your own business, the plan can help you make the correct choices before putting your savings into a costly new business.

Great ideas come when we're sitting around chatting with others. When you are writing your business plan, talk with family and friends in both formal and informal brainstorming sessions. These sessions can be useful for solving specific problems and for getting creative ideas in business planning. Make lists, including the pros and cons of working from your kitchen. Is there a market for your product? Are you capable of working from your home kitchen?

You may know immediately how big or small you want your business to be. Maybe you want to keep it small, with enough restrictions to fit your business around your lifestyle. Maybe what you really want is to have a large operation that can support your entire family. Maybe you don't know yet. It's good to be aware of your present personal limits and any future options. Once you have created your business plan, keep it close by so you can add to it or change aspects of it as your business grows.

When you create your business plan, make sure it is easy to read, especially if you want investors for your business. Your plan should have separate headings for each section and no typos. Make it as professional as possible.

The following sections are usually included in a conventional business plan.

1. Executive Summary

The executive summary is the first (and most important) element of a business plan. It's an overview or outline of the entire plan and should be no longer than one page.

If your intended reader is an investor or bank lender, concentrate on the projected finances in your executive summary. Since the summary incorporates information from all the other sections, it is easier if you write this part *after* you have completed writing the rest of the business plan.

2. Statement of Purpose

The statement of purpose is also known as the mission statement. It defines your central values and goals. It explains what your business does in a few words or a couple of sentences. Be as concise as possible.

3. History and Background

The history and background section is very important if you're hoping for a bank loan or appealing to investors, even if the investors are friends or family. It shows your background and discusses your food-related and business experience.

In this section, describe your skills, experience, education (e.g., degree, classes taken, workshops), and previous employment. Emphasize any past jobs in or related to the food industry. If food has been only a hobby up until now, add that here. If you have an extensive résumé that directly relates to this business, include or attach it to the business plan.

4. Description of the Business and Products

The description of the business and products covers several issues. It discusses the name of your business, its location, and the products you plan to sell.

Include the name of your business, why you chose that name, and how it will attract customers. You will also want to add the business address or location. If it's in your home, briefly state that you will have an inspected, legal kitchen. If you will be using another kitchen, discuss the facilities included and mention any support that is offered. Also note where your bookkeeping and business office will be located.

Review the products you plan to offer and why you chose those products. You can also list your ideas for future products. Discuss your delivery methods and how products will get to customers. You can briefly describe your target customers and why they will choose your products over your competitors'. This is especially important if you are looking at a niche business such as special diet foods or meal parts for home delivery.

5. Company Values

The company values section describes how you want your company to be viewed by the public. Talk about the kind of product line you plan to offer and the overall idea behind your product choices. Will you bake homemade goodies or products that are for a special diet?

If you have a company theme — for instance, you only use ecologically friendly products or you promote recycling — add that information. If you are involved in community activities related to your business, add that in this section as well.

6. Operations and Employees

The operations and employees section discusses the structure and operations of your business. You can begin this section by talking about who will run the business. For example, will the business be owned and run by you alone, or will you have a partner?

If you need employees, discuss your recruitment and training methods, the pay structure, and the requisite skill level for your employees. State if you will hire them yourself, or if you plan to use a temporary hiring service. If an outside service is used, give your reasons for this; bookkeeping may be simpler, or if you only need seasonal help, it may make more sense to use a temporary agency.

7. Market Research

The first thing you need to describe in the market research section of your business plan is your target market. Will your customers be retail customers, wholesale customers, or both? Retail is where you sell directly to the consumer. Wholesale means that you sell your products to businesses that resell your products to their consumers. (For more information on retail and wholesale customers, see Chapter 9.) Why have you targeted this area of consumer?

Discuss what market research you have done and break it into primary and secondary categories. Primary research is the work that you have done to gather information, such as doing informal surveys of potential customers or visiting stores to see what your potential competition is doing. Use your notes — add dates and list the places you visited — to show that you really have done the research.

Secondary research includes looking at materials and data that have been collected by others. Places to look for this information include libraries, trade associations, and local business groups. List anything else that you've done, such as looking through the phone book for potential competitors, searching the Internet, reading magazines, and studying this book. If you have a subscription to a trade magazine, add that here as well.

In this section, you may also talk about your potential competition. Include information about who they are, what they sell, and what makes your products different. What sets you apart? Be as specific as possible.

8. Promotional Strategies

The promotional strategies section describes how you will target and develop a customer base, how the business will be marketed, and if you will participate in any community activities to promote your business.

List the activities you will do to promote your business, such as creating flyers and brochures for distribution at public markets or making guest appearances on local radio and cable shows. For additional promotional ideas, read Chapter 10.

9. Financing and Start-up Expenses

If you're appealing to potential financiers for start-up capital, the finance and start-up expenses section will be the most important element of the plan. This area shows potential backers that you are serious about making the business profitable. Your lenders want to know they will be paid back, so there must be enough details in this section for them to feel confident that they will have their investment returned.

Include how much you will need for start-up, how you will acquire it, how long it will take to make a profit, and how much of your own money will be invested. You will need to speak in terms that bankers understand, so include graphs and charts. You may want to consider hiring a professional to help you create this section.

This section may also include spreadsheets to predict future monthly projections. Your market research data, along with how much you think you can produce and sell within your projected business operation, will help you fill in the numbers. Build any seasonal fluctuations into your forecast. This section should give you an understanding of how much business you need to do in order to make a profit.

When I hoped to move my bakery business from a rental site and purchase a building for a bakery café concept, I needed financing. At that time, bakeries and cafés were an unusual pairing. I asked my tax accountant for help with my financial plan and he put together an extensive outline. He sent it to three banks and from that information, one of the banks, with the backing of the Small Business Administration (SBA) and the city's development office, provided the loan. Without an in-depth business plan, getting the loans would have been impossible.

10. Projections and Forecasts

If you plan to keep your company in business for many years, you may want to make a forecast of where you want to be in the next three to five years. This helps you keep focused on your goals as your business grows. For example, you may need to set aside money quarterly in order to move your business from your home into a retail location in two years.

Revisiting your plan annually will help you to know if you are on track with your goals. If you are off track, your business plan can help you get refocused.

11. Personal Business Plan

Take a look at Sample 2 for a simplified personal business plan. This plan is good for when you are starting your business in your home. Notice that this simplified version strays somewhat from the points listed in the previous sections. It's intended to help you understand and focus on what's important and what you need to do to get your business started. It will make you think about questions you might not have thought about.

If you need investors, then you will need to create a more detailed plan using the information outlined in sections **1.** through **10.**

As you read through this book, you will understand more and can fill in the Business Plan worksheet located on the CD. First, write some general ideas for your basic planning, add issues you will need to address, and leave lots of space for the answers you don't yet know.

12. Business Planning Help

If you're nervous about starting a business and need some coaching or one-on-one help, both the United States and Canada have small business groups offering no-cost programs and services. Small Business Development Centers can be found across both countries. The Resources section on the CD has links to more information for both US and Canadian businesses.

In the United States there are online classes and individualized mentors from the Service Corp of Retired Executives (SCORE) to help you succeed. They're a partnership involving the federal and local government and they have low cost or free business training.

In Canada, you can contact Canada Business, which gives up-to-date and accurate business information as well as provides referrals to government services, regulations, and programs. Additionally, Self-Counsel Press has a book titled *Starting a Successful Business in Canada*, which contains lots of helpful advice for new business owners.

Be wary of businesses or websites that tell you how to become rich if you pay for their products or advice. I came across a few of them while researching this book. If they scream about how much they can help, and how wonderfully awesome they are, let temptation pass. They're small businesses too, and the only thing they want to help is *their own* bank accounts!

SIMPLIFIED BUSINESS PLAN

Business Name and Address
The Cookie Tree
8491 Our Development
Anywhere, Anystate, USA 55555
(555) 555-5555
CutieCookie123@internet.com
TheCookieTree@cookies.com

Sole Proprietor
Careen Cookie
Address same as above

Statement of Purpose
To provide delicious, all-natural, healthy cookies to the local community.

Products
Cookies of every type and variety, using fresh ingredients.

Customers
Retail sales at the local farmers' markets and to neighbors. Wholesale to the local schools, college cafeterias, and small neighborhood markets. My business will make all deliveries.

Promotional Strategies
Flyers distributed to neighborhood mailboxes and for farmers' market sales. Business cards and a separate wholesale price list to give to school purchasing agents and area markets.

Operations and Employees
Will bake in my kitchen with occasional help from family members. Cookies will be either individually wrapped or packaged in bags of one dozen, for delivery three times per week. Husband promises to make deliveries, but contingency plan in place. Store shelf and counter display will be my responsibility.

Market Research
Local schools and colleges only sell prewrapped factory cookies. Neighborhood markets sell prepackaged all-natural (not fresh!) cookies made in a national factory. Three other home bakers currently selling at farmers' market, but only one makes cookies and none of the bakers use all-natural ingredients.

Suppliers
Ingredient supplies purchased from local food co-op and natural food stores (they have agreed to give me a discount); also from supermarkets. Paper goods and other packaging purchased from regional supplier and local dollar stores.

Financing and Start-up Expenses
Only need enough to cover ingredients and paper, packaging, and office supplies. I have $300 in savings, plus possible short-term loans from several hungry friends and neighbors. Currently working on an agreement in which they each pay me $50 in return for a coupon to be exchanged later for custom cookies.

Sour Cream Coffee Cake

Preheat oven to 350°F and prepare two standard loaf pans with spray or paper liners.

Cream the butter or margarine with sugar. Beat in the eggs and vanilla; mix in the sour cream.

Add flour, baking soda, and salt. Mix until thoroughly combined. This should be a very thick batter; add more flour if necessary. Be careful not to overmix; doing so makes the loaf tough and creates large air holes.

Refrigerate what you will not use immediately; stir additions into remaining batter.

Fill loaf tins about 2/3 high and bake for 20 to 60 minutes, depending on size. When done, the top will be brown, the sides will pull away from the tin, and when gently pressed, the top will remain firm with no finger imprint.

Cool thoroughly before icing or storing. Baked loaf remains fresh for several days at room temperature, two weeks in fridge, or six months in freezer. Batter keeps for one week stored in fridge. Stir before using.

For variations of this recipe see the file on the CD:

Coffee, Bundt, and Pound Cakes

Yield: two small loaves

1 cup (2 sticks) butter or margarine

2 cups granulated sugar

5 large eggs

1 tablespoon vanilla extract

2 cups (1 pint) sour cream

5 cups all-purpose flour, approximately

1 tablespoon baking soda

1 teaspoon salt

Optional additions: chopped fresh or dried fruit, nuts, or chocolate chips

Chapter 4
Making Your Business Legal

Once you start selling goods, you're running a business. To make it a legal business, there are some basic things you need to do. If you're not the business type, it can feel overwhelming to look at the entire scope of the coming venture. That's exactly how I felt. I hated the business end and only wanted to bake. But as I began checking off steps on my business to-do list, it felt good to know I was making progress.

If the legal business part scares you, read through this chapter and move on; but reread it when you are ready to make your business legal. Of course, you can always decide to work outside the law and take your chances. Working "under the table" can seem initially appealing because there's no keeping track of anything and no annoying paperwork or regulations to deal with. However, there are several reasons for going legit:

- You can fully participate in any venue you choose and not be restricted based on your nonlegal status.

- There are opportunities to grow that are not available to illegitimate businesses (e.g., moving to a retail storefront or doing business with clients that need your business license).

- Not being afraid that someone (most often a competitor) will report you to the authorities.

- Having a permanent record of your success so if you ever want to sell your business, you could make a profit from all your hard work.

1. Your Business Structure

To begin your business, you can start off simple and create a sole proprietorship, or start your business with someone else and create a partnership. There are many other business structures; however, this book is meant to help you start a home-based business, so it only includes information about sole proprietorships and partnerships. If you would like more information about other business structures, Self-Counsel Press publishes *How to Form and Operate a Limited Liability Company* in the US, and in Canada, the *Incorporation Guide for Canada*.

1.1 Sole proprietorship

The simplest form of business is the sole proprietorship. It's a one-person business structure and takes the least amount of time, money, and paperwork to set up. For income tax purposes, the sole proprietor declares all the profits as income on his or her individual tax returns, and files any tax forms related to owning a business.

The sole proprietor is responsible for all the debt and shoulders all the risks, with unlimited liability. Financing for this form of business is more difficult to obtain because of the risk to lenders.

In the US, depending where you live, you may have to pay special fees and obtain a business license and/or a seller's permit to collect taxes. Your business is automatically a sole proprietorship if you do not form a partnership or corporation. Contact the Internal Revenue Service (IRS) for more information.

In Canada, there are minimal requirements for setting up a sole proprietorship. You must get a Certificate of Compliance, a business license, and register for a business name. You may also have to register for the Goods and Services Tax (GST), Provincial Sales Tax (PST), or Harmonized Sales Tax (HST). Taxes are reported on the personal tax return, which must include a financial statement. Contact Canada Revenue Agency (CRA) for more information.

1.2 Partnership

A business with more than one owner is a partnership. Setting up the partnership is similar to setting up a sole proprietorship.

In the US, there may be special fees associated with a partnership, and you may be required to obtain a business license and/or a seller's permit to collect taxes. Filing taxes requires that each partner report their share of profit or loss on their individual tax returns. Contact the IRS for more information.

In Canada, there are minimal registration requirements. As with a sole proprietorship, the partners must obtain a Certificate of Compliance, a business license, and register for a business name. You may also need to register for GST, PST, or HST. Each partner declares his or her share of the partnership income or loss on an individual personal income tax return. Each partner will also have to file an individual financial statement. Contact CRA for more information.

When two or more people go into a business partnership, especially when neither has any business experience, certain key issues can arise. Early discussions should center on how each partner envisions where the business will go and what their respective roles in the business will be. Will each partner put in the same number of hours? How will the money be divided? Even when they've been friends for a long time, a business relationship can put a strain on the friendship and eventually turn the business sour. Set up some rules and remember that some issues may seem insurmountable, but compromises and creative thinking can often turn bad situations into good ones.

If you are considering a partnership, you should prepare a legally written partnership agreement. This agreement should outline how much time, money, and work each partner will contribute. It could also include agreements regarding the division of labor, decision-making process, resolution of disputes, and partnership dissolution. Having a partnership agreement helps if any issues do arise. For help on preparing a partnership agreement, Self-Counsel Press publishes a *Partnership Agreement* kit in the Forms on CD series.

2. Choose a Business Name

Every business needs a name, so start making a list. Your business name speaks for you and should immediately identify your purpose. It's the first thing people will know about your business.

Brainstorm names that are self-explanatory so people know immediately that you're in the business of food. Ask friends and family for suggestions. Write down food words and phrases, and use the dictionary and thesaurus for inspiration. If you want a homey feel, include a first or last name or family designation, but try to go a step better than generic. *Grandma's Cookies* and *Mom's Cakes* are okay, but not special. A memorable name for a cake decorating business might be *Susan's Slice of Heaven*.

When deciding on a name, think long term. You'll want a name that you can keep as your business grows. Don't pick a name that will limit your product line, such as *Mystical Muffins*. When you decide to change it later to *Mystical Muffins and More*, it will stick in customers' minds that you only make muffins. *Susan's Slice of Heaven* is still a great name because it can incorporate more than just cake slices.

Another point to consider when choosing a name is to find something easy to pronounce and simple to spell so customers can easily find you in the phone book or on the Internet.

2.1 Register your business name

If you will be doing business under a name that is not your legal name, such as *Old Town Bakery* instead of *Smith's Bakery*, you are working under a fictitious business name. In the US and Canada, a fictitious business name is also known as Doing Business As (DBA), assumed business name, Trading As (t/a), or trade styles.

In order to run your business under the assumed name, you must complete and register a DBA form. This is a simple process that can be done through your local courthouse, county or state office, or government registry. The clerk will check to make sure the name is not already in use in your county. Registration will ensure that no other business in your licensing locality can use your business name. This protection only extends to your county. Blank forms are available free through many localities, or can be purchased in an office supply or legal supply store.

In some areas you will be required to publish the business name in your local newspaper for a specified period of time. In these areas, you are required to do this to inform the public of your intent to operate under a fictitious name. When you register your business name, find out what requirements are necessary for using an assumed name in your area.

It is important to note that if you want to open a business bank account under your assumed business name, or want to deposit checks made out to your business, you may need to obtain a DBA form in order to open the account.

If you're hoping to expand the business, it would be wise to do a trademark search (see Resources on the CD for links to trademark information) before settling on a name. You may also want to check for domain names so you can reserve a website.

3. Employer Identification Number or Business Number

Most businesses are required to get an Employer Identification Number (EIN) in the US, or a Business Number (BN) in Canada. These are numbers used to identify a business; their purpose is similar to that of a Social Security

Number (SSN) or a Social Insurance Number (SIN).

Any business type other than a sole proprietorship must get an EIN or a BN. Sole proprietors without employees can simply use their SSN or SIN, but it is advisable to get an EIN or a BN. If you are going to hire employees, then an EIN or a BN is required.

The EIN or BN assigned to your business will be used by the IRS or CRA to keep track of the amount of taxes you pay. In the US, you may also be required to get a state Employer Identification Number from the state in which you are doing business. This is so they can also keep track of the amount of state taxes you are paying. Contact your state tax department for more information on state tax requirements.

In the US, to get an EIN, contact the IRS and complete and file the applicable forms. In Canada, you can contact the CRA to set up your company's CRA account and file a Request for a Business Number.

4. Business License and Seller's Permit

To protect the consumer, some local governments regulate and keep track of businesses by requiring that businesses acquire a business license. This license is separate from the health permit for food production. Contact your county, city, state, or provincial offices and ask for the local business license requirements. Also, if you want to have a business bank account, you must have a business license.

You may also be required to obtain a seller's permit for tax collection purposes. In the US, this permit is sometimes called a Certificate of Resale, or Certificate of Authority. You can get a seller's permit from your state or city tax department in the locality where you are going to operate your business.

In Canada, the provinces and territories each have different rules about seller's permits. If you would like more information, talk to the clerk at your local municipal government office.

5. Food Production License

You'll need a health permit for your kitchen. If you're using another facility, you may be operating under their permit. Contact your county clerk's office or local health department to find out the agency responsible for a food production license, or refer to the listings in the Resources on the CD.

For the most part, the health department rules are meant to protect the consumer and are not unduly difficult to follow. It may seem easier to skip this step, but remember, if you bake without a license, anyone has the power to turn you in. Eventually someone, usually your competition, may find out and alert the authorities.

I read about a woman operating her strawberry dipping business from home when a competitor turned her in to the health department. This scare was enough to prompt her to begin using a licensed facility, but sometimes being reported forces a business to close down permanently.

Someday another business will come along and undercut your prices because they slid by the rules. Then you may be the one who wants to get rid of this unfair competition.

5.1 Food production license and legal issues

With food processing regulations, every locality is different. In some places there are no restrictions on using a home kitchen and no food-handling license is necessary. In many areas, the licensing agency only allows certain kinds of production in a home kitchen. For other places still, a separate kitchen in the home must be used. The rules vary from place to place, so you must find out which agency in your area does the licensing.

To get you underway, the Resources file on the CD has a list of contacts pertaining to business licenses. You could begin by calling your local health department and asking about the guidelines for home kitchen processing. The department will direct you to the appropriate authority.

Whether or not you require a license for your kitchen depends on different factors in different areas. In some areas it depends on what type of food processing is done, while in other areas it depends on how much income is generated by your business. In some areas, certain types of food processing are allowed while others are not. For example, home-canned foods might not be allowed, while candy or baking is okay.

The official line might be that catering is prohibited while certain types of food processing are allowed. If you run into this issue, make sure the authority defines "catering." In my area the county health department inspects retail kitchen facilities (i.e., restaurants, delis, supermarkets) and does not allow for any home catering or home food processing. But the State Department of Agriculture and Markets inspects wholesale facilities and small home-based businesses. They restrict production to certain types of foods that do not require special handling or refrigeration, such as bakery items (e.g., cookies, cakes, and granolas). Meat and cheese items that require refrigeration, including cheesecake, are not allowed. As long as I have basic necessities such as plumbing (i.e., hot and cold running water), I'm using a clean work area (no working from a lean-to behind a chicken coop), and meet a few other minor requirements, I'm in business.

Contact your local authorities and follow the rules. Remember that this is not only about you and your needs — it's also about keeping consumers safe and healthy. Rules are meant to protect the customer, and a happy customer spreads the word. Plus, there are many venues that will be closed to you if you do not have a license. Farmers' markets, restaurants, and delis are all public areas and you will not be allowed to sell there without a baking permit.

It's additionally important to work from a legally acceptable kitchen, or your business will always be susceptible to that knock on the door. If you're only baking and selling to coworkers, that's not as open to scrutiny as giving out flyers and soliciting business from strangers. If you bake without a license, anyone has the ability to turn you in. Eventually, a mean-spirited neighbor, or your competition, will find out and alert the authorities. There are enough things to worry about in running your own business without worrying that you will be found out and ordered to close down immediately.

A special note for anyone still wanting to immediately jump in and remodel: Some localities will only license a kitchen if it's not used for personal family meals. Sometimes a basement area or a garage can be renovated without too much investment. If you are tentative about this venture and not quite sure it would work for you, it might make more sense to rent production space from a licensed facility.

6. Insurance

Check with your home insurance agent before starting up your business. There are different kinds of insurance policies, and your home insurance may not be adequate to carry a home-based business without additional cost. You're in a low-risk business, so you need to weigh the risks against the amount it costs to have the insurance. Common sense should help you decide.

Homeowners' insurance (or renters' insurance) will cover a home kitchen business, but you will need a rider, a special "endorsement," to receive the coverage. For liability insurance that covers your products, you must purchase commercial insurance, sometimes called a vendor policy. Call your insurance agent for more information.

7. Zoning Laws

Zoning laws are meant to ensure that neighborhoods aren't turned into commercial areas with excessive traffic. If you already live in a rural area, a commercial district, or on a busy road, it should be relatively easy to get a variance. If, however, you live in a residential area, you will need to make promises that your small business will not create additional traffic. These assurances may include that you will do no retail business from your house; you will have no customers flooding your street; you will not post signs; you will make your own deliveries; and very few, if any, trucks will make deliveries to your home.

Almond Chocolate Chip Cookies

Preheat oven to 375°F and line cookie sheets with foil or parchment.

Cream together the butter, shortening, almond paste, and sugar. Mix in the egg and extract.

Add the flour, baking powder, and salt. Mix until dough is fully blended. This will be a stiff dough.

Mix in the chocolate chips and nuts (if using). If the dough is too stiff for your mixer, use your hands or a wooden spoon.

Drop dough at least 2 inches apart and bake for 10 to 15 minutes, depending on size, until the bottoms are a light golden brown and the tops of the cookies appear dry and cracked.

Cool before storing. Keeps for up to one week at room temperature or for six months in the freezer.

For variations of this recipe see the file on the CD:

Cookies

Yield: 1½ dozen large or 4-5 dozen small cookies

½ cup (1 stick) butter, softened

½ cup shortening

½ cup almond paste

1 cup granulated sugar

1 large egg

1½ teaspoons almond extract

2 cups all-purpose flour

¾ teaspoon baking powder

½ teaspoon salt

1 cup (6 oz bag) semisweet chocolate chips

Optional: ½ cup chopped almonds

Chapter 5
Financial Management

It's a good idea to keep your finances organized from the beginning. Here are a few reasons why:

- You will know if anyone owes you money and if you owe anyone money.

- You will know how much money you're making.

- You will be prepared for tax time.

- If you want to borrow money, you will have proof of your business growth.

- If you sell your business, you will have proof of the business income.

Understanding your income and expenses is important to keep your business running smoothly. This chapter will help you get started on the right track to financial business success.

1. Start-up Capital

Start-up capital is the amount of money needed to get your business started. In order to figure out how much start-up capital you need, you first have to make a few decisions about the products you will offer, the ingredients and packaging you must have, and if you need any equipment to start production.

No matter if you have a small amount or a large amount of money to begin your business, the following three approaches will help you get started.

1.1 Minimalist approach

Even if you're on a very small budget and borrowing money is not an option, you can begin a home-based business. Your overhead (e.g., monthly expenses for rent and utilities) is already part of your living expenses, and you can probably scrape by with your current kitchen appliances, so all you'll need to get started is enough for the business license, health permit, and purchasing supplies (e.g., ingredients, packaging, and labels). If you sell at a market, you might need to pay a vendor fee for a booth or table.

If you are using the minimalist approach to starting your business, you should choose a product that can be made with the appliances you already own. If your basic equipment is not working, either review the product lists in Chapter 2 or beg, borrow, or trade to have a stove and refrigerator in working order.

I nervously began with the minimalist approach and borrowed $200 from my checking account, which was money I needed to pay bills. I purchased a used oven through an ad in the local *Pennysaver*, paid for my licenses, bought equipment I didn't already have (i.e., large spatulas and a huge, plastic baby bathtub for mixing), and borrowed cookie sheets from friends. I had enough money left to purchase ingredients for my first baking session. My labels were hand printed shelf signs for two accounts (a local food co-op and a small grocery store) and I delivered bread, granola, and large cookies twice a week. The money from my first few deliveries bought more ingredients and after a month I was able to repay the "loan" and buy yet more ingredients. In the following months I bought a few miscellaneous baking pans and slowly continued increasing my product line and outlets. It would have been easier and faster to grow my business if I'd had the initial funds to buy everything, but I had to be resourceful in the beginning.

1.2 Moderate approach

If you have some savings as a resource, excellent! If you don't, but have devoted friends and relatives, great! Take your business plan that you prepared after reading Chapter 3, which includes your product list, your desired equipment and ingredients, and your miscellaneous needs. Invite hopefully generous family or friends to your new business headquarters. Solicit their financial help.

Make sure you put everything in writing — when and how much you are borrowing, when you will repay it, and if there will be any interest. Your friends and family realize they are taking a risk, and they will be pleasantly surprised when you hand them an agreement with all the terms.

A variation of this approach is to make the contracts for small amounts of money, to be given to as many people as necessary until you raise the amount you want. See Sample 3 for a brief, fun way to write up the contract. On the CD you will find a Repayment Contract Worksheet to help you prepare your own contract.

SAMPLE 3
REPAYMENT CONTRACT

Thanks for your encouragement!

Starting a new business is always hard, but with your financial help I am off to a great start. As per our agreement, I am borrowing $100. This will be repaid in four monthly installments of $25 beginning six months from the date we sign this contract. Interest will be paid in baked goods, one dozen cookies to accompany each installment, flavor to be chosen by my wonderful financial backer.

Date:
Borrower's signature:
Lender's signature:

SELF-COUNSEL PRESS — START & RUN A HOME-BASED FOOD BUSINESS 09

Another fun variation is to sell coupons for a specified amount of money to be repaid with goods only. Create terms for the exchange — for example, a coupon worth $5 can be sold for $4 (that's a 25 percent interest rate), and your "investors" can "buy" your products after a specified date when you are already in production. Put the exchange terms on the coupon or contract to avoid later misunderstandings. See Sample 4. On the CD, there is an Investor Coupon Worksheet to help you create your own coupon.

1.3 Flush-with-capital approach

If you do have enough capital to get started, your biggest danger lies in spending too much for things you don't need. Having money to start a business can make a person giddy. Go ahead and order fancy packaging for those decorated cookies, but don't renovate your kitchen if you —

- have never owned or managed a business,
- have never worked in a food environment and are not familiar with equipment,
- don't like kitchen work,
- have a habit of moving from one uncompleted project to the next, or
- have a family with other priorities.

If you are sure you are ready, test the business by making as few changes to your home as the health law will allow, or rent a space and try it for a year. Do you really want to rip apart your kitchen and put in expensive equipment that might remind you next year of your

SAMPLE 4
INVESTOR COUPON

$$ $$$ Investor Coupon $$$ $$

This coupon costs $10 (early bird special, $8).

Exchange this coupon for $12 worth of baked goods to be ordered from my future product list. (One-week notice, please.)

May be redeemed anytime after six months from date below.

Date: _____

Borrower's Signature: _____

Investor's Signature: _____

failure? Start small, even when you have the funds to start big.

2. Bookkeeping: Keep Track of Your Business

Bookkeeping is an essential part of running a business. Keep track of both your income and your expenses so that your records reflect the money you make from your sales, along with the expenses of running your business.

There's no law or requirement for how a business keeps records, but in order to report your finances to the government, you must have a certain amount of information. It's not difficult once you get started, but it can be frustrating when you already have lots to do. You do have choices. Your bookkeeping method can be relatively simple when compared to that of a traditional business. You don't have to do a profit and loss statement, make projections, or create a fancy spreadsheet. If you collect the necessary information to meet the basic requirements for paying taxes, you don't have to worry about anything else. Do whatever level of bookkeeping that makes and keeps your business running, in a way that makes you feel comfortable.

My first few years in business, before computers were around, I had a handwritten ledger for expenses. At the end of each month I totaled the columns and at the end of each year I totaled the months. After years of using a pencil so I could easily erase mistakes, I was told that I must use a pen so the auditors don't see any eraser marks. Luckily, no one ever asked to see my records, but now I use a pen just in case.

In addition to the expense ledger, I kept a separate book for retail and wholesale income. With these figures I was able to do my own taxes. After several years, although I continued to keep my own business ledgers, I had a tax professional use my figures for filing taxes.

There are now many good software programs designed for a small business. If you don't feel you are ready for a computer software program, you can purchase a paper ledger, which is a book designed for business purposes. Office supply stores sell inexpensive paper ledgers with between 2 and 13 columns. Recording your business income will be relatively easy. Create a computer file or spreadsheet, use a small notebook, or a sheet of paper. The point is to have a simple and easily completed system that works for you. It's not difficult to keep track of your finances, but you must keep up with the entries or it can get unmanageable and overwhelming.

You can do all this yourself by following the methods described here, or have a bookkeeper or an accountant help you set up a system. From this bookkeeping, you can then do your own business tax forms at the end of each year or pay for the services of a tax preparer.

2.1 Business expenses and deductions

Most business expenses can be deducted from your business income so that you pay taxes only on the difference between income and expenses. This is great incentive to make sure you record all the expenses you are allowed to deduct by the government. The important thing to remember with deductions is to save and file all your expense receipts.

Large equipment is amortized, which means instead of deducting the entire cost at once, you deduct smaller amounts each year over the period of time specified by your government agency. This category can get fairly confusing for anyone other than an accountant. For a small home-based food business, you will rarely need this category. However, if your business grows or you are buying large equipment, you should consider hiring an accountant.

Any expense that is a necessary part of your goods (e.g., ingredients and packaging) is tax deductible. Expenses directly related to your business that are strictly business related, such as seeking professional tax advice or printing product flyers, are also deductible. Rent you pay for the use of another kitchen is also tax deductible.

In the US, if you use a home kitchen, and it is a *separate* second facility in your home that is used *strictly* for business, or you have designated storage space in your home which is only used for business supplies, those are allowable deductions. However, if your business uses your home kitchen and you prepare family meals in the same kitchen using the same equipment, this is not an allowable expense. Any purchase that might be construed as personal, such as a new oven for your family kitchen, a computer (even if used on a minimal level for nonbusiness purposes), or a new dining room table, is not deductible unless you are willing to prove that those are used strictly for business. You may not deduct a percentage of your mortgage, rent, or utilities. Note that the Internal Revenue Service (IRS) uses the term "regular and exclusive" to apply to a deductible business expense. For more information about tax deductions, contact the IRS.

In Canada, the rules for deductions are different than those in the US. If a space is used primarily for your home-based business, you may be able to deduct a portion of your household expenses that directly relate to operating your business. These deductions can include lights, water, heat, maintenance, telephone, and Internet fees. If you rent your home, a portion of the rent may be deducted. If you

own your home, you may be able to claim a portion of your mortgage interest (note: not the mortgage payments themselves), property taxes, and insurance. For more information about business-use-of-home deductions, contact Canada Revenue Agency (CRA).

If you make any potentially questionable deductions, make sure you document with pictures and receipts, and be prepared for an audit.

For recording expenses in your ledger, you need at least five columns per page to record monthly amounts. More columns depends on the size of your business and how detailed your categories are. (See Sample 5.) The CD includes a Monthly Expense Ledger Worksheet to help you create your own ledger.

Note: The miscellaneous column in the sample was not totaled because the entries are not in the major categories and will therefore be listed separately at the end of the year.

You can break down the expenses however you like, but the more detailed and narrow the category, the easier it will be to use those numbers when doing your tax return. With more details transcribed at the outset, at the end of the year you may only need to total the 12 months.

Each purchase should have a corresponding receipt. Your entries can have a brief notation about the purchase, such as where your supplies were bought or what equipment needed repair. The notation helps if you need to find the corresponding receipt at a later date.

When you're shopping, it simplifies bookkeeping if you do not mix personal family food with business ingredients. Keep your business food on separate receipts. It also simplifies bookkeeping if you separate food purchases from other supplies, since these purchases need separate ledger totals. You can certainly put

MONTHLY EXPENSE LEDGER

Date March 20--	Ingredients	Packaging	Office Supplies	Fees, Licenses, Permits	Mileage	Miscellaneous*
1		$37.68 Dan Brothers	$3.40 stamps		11 miles	
2	$128.97 supermarket				6 miles	
4	$46.29 discount store			$40 annual license		
6			$68.19 Office Supply Depot			
9	$14.68 Target				5 miles	$23.09 hand towels Target
12	$51.22 supermarket			$100 market vendor season	4 miles	
15		$29.51 Dan Brothers			9 miles	
16	$147.87 supermarket				6 miles	$110 tax preparer
25						$87 Jackson Plumbing
27	$6.92 Target	$26.97 Target (Easter supplies)			5 miles	
30	$125.48 supermarket				6 miles	
Total	**$521.43**	**$94.16**	**$71.59**	**$140.00**	**52 miles**	

everything on one store receipt, but later when you make entries you'll need to spend time dividing the receipt amounts instead of taking the totals directly from your receipts.

These are the usual expenses involved in running a home-based food business:

- Cost of goods: all ingredients that go into making your products.

- Packaging supplies: labels, bags, boxes, doilies, food wrap; anything that becomes part of your sale.

- Office expenses: paper, pens, postage, ledger, receipt books.

- Licenses, permits, and any business fees, including vendor permits.

Some of the following categories may also apply to you:

- Vehicle expenses: keep a separate mileage log with dates, purpose, and destinations.

- Advertising and promotional materials, including printing services for flyers or brochures.

- Legal and professional services such as accounting, legal, and all consulting services.

- Rent, if using another facility.

- Repairs and maintenance (covers equipment and appliance problems resulting from the running of your business).

- Insurance for your business, if any.

- Professional dues and trade journal subscriptions.

- Equipment leases, if any.

- Uniforms and towels: cost of anything you purchased (e.g., aprons or hand towels) and approximately how much it costs each week or month to do the laundry.

- Wages: any payment for labor, whether you do the bookkeeping yourself or go through a service.

- Donations (but check for current tax guidelines).

2.1a Saving receipts

Remember, save all your receipts and set aside time every week to enter the amounts in your ledger and income files. After you have finished recording the receipt amounts, place each receipt in a designated place. You can keep them in an envelope, clipped together and put in a shoebox, or, for the best organization, file them in a filing cabinet with separate files for the different types of expenses. If you keep them in chronological order, it will make your life easier come tax time.

Do whatever seems best and easiest for you. Just make sure to do it. This will help you to be organized.

2.2 Business income

To record income, use a small-business software program, a spreadsheet, a little paper book, or the Monthly Income Record Worksheet (included on the CD). Post the income amounts on a regular basis — the more sales you have, the more often you should post. Keep wholesale and retail sales separate. This makes sales tax easier to identify. Keep copies of all your sales receipts clearly marked as retail or wholesale. For more information on wholesale and retail sales see Chapter 9.

For record-keeping purposes, write a sales receipt for each of your wholesale transactions. Give the wholesaler a copy and keep the other copy in the receipt book. You can purchase little receipt books with duplicate or triplicate sheets in office supply stores. I also suggest (if possible) that you put all your accounts on cash on delivery (COD).

Retail sales are different. If you have multiple retail sales in one day (e.g., you sell at the market or have a delivery route), total the entire amount for the day and enter the total under the date, with a separate column for sales tax.

In a store with a cash register, every purchase is automatically recorded on the receipt tape, but no one would expect you to record every single cookie or muffin sale at the market. Your handwritten notes should be enough. You might want to give sales receipts to some retail customers, especially if you have a delivery route, to help you stay organized.

Again, there's no rule for how you keep these records, as long as you can produce whatever a tax auditor might ask to see if the IRS or CRA are ever interested.

See Sample 6 for an example of an income record. Please note that all retail amounts are either to the dollar or 50 cents because I use a price structure to avoid sales needing excessive change.

For keeping copies of your sales receipts, a shoebox, envelope, or file folder is fine. Make sure you keep your income records separate from your expense receipts to save you from later confusion. My business included more wholesale business than retail so within the box I kept clearly marked envelopes for each wholesale account and one envelope for all retail sales. When my envelope got too thick I started another one. I stored the envelopes in a box and used a different box each year.

2.2a Collecting payment

When you're running a small business, the best wholesale accounts are ones that pay at the time of delivery. However, many businesses or wholesale accounts don't want to pay when they receive an order, instead preferring to be billed weekly or monthly.

With each order, always include a sales invoice and have someone sign for it. Make a note if the order has been paid. Leave your copy of the invoice in the receipt book (or if creating your own invoices, print a second copy for yourself). When you have been paid, enter the amount in your income book. Follow up immediately on past due bills. Always check your books — if you haven't been paid by the agreed time, send the payor an invoice total. That's why having records is so nice — your memory is not solely responsible for keeping track.

Be wary of accounts that want you to extend further credit. Even the largest companies have financial issues and try to use their power to not pay bills. Practice saying, "Sorry, I'm sure you can appreciate that we are a small business and depend on prompt payment." Restaurants are notorious for running up large bills and eventually going out of business owing creditors. They will be great when starting a relationship but once you have a working agreement they can begin dragging their feet. Then suddenly one day you read in the paper that they have been closed down or they have declared bankruptcy.

If you decide to extend credit, set a limit. I once had a restaurant that initially paid within ten working days, then slowly their payments lagged and eventually their bill was up to $500. I was tipped off by my supply sales rep that the restaurant was having trouble. I was a single mom and that money was needed to pay my bills. "So sorry," I said when the restaurant placed the next order, "but now it's cash only." Luckily for me, they paid the past due balance and continued paying COD. Two months later they closed and I was not one of their creditors. Businesses don't set out wanting to cheat suppliers or vendors, it just sometimes happens. That's part of the downside to the business world.

For retail sales, cash is the simplest form of payment. Make sure to always have lots of change on hand.

Almost everyone uses credit cards today. Be aware that there's an additional cost for the vendor. Set a minimum amount or give a discount for cash purchases. For the ability to accept credit cards, ask your bank representative.

Be careful about taking personal checks. Petty criminals know that small-business owners can be naive to their tricks, and won't come after the criminals or prosecute for small amounts. If the customer acts disinterested about prices and/or acts as if cost is no object, then probably cost *is* no object because the person has no intentions of ever paying for your goods. You have the right to refuse a check or

MONTHLY INCOME RECORD

Date: October 20--	Retail	Taxable retail, if applicable	Wholesale
1			$15 Benny's Deli $38 Chesapeake Cafe
2	$87.50 farmers' market		
3			
4			
5	$97.50 office delivery		$12 Benny's Deli
6			
7	$61 office delivery $250 balance, Danker wedding cake		
8			$16 Benny's Deli $95 Chesapeake Cafe
9	$96.50 farmers' market		
10			
11			
12	$85 office delivery		$23 Benny's Deli
13			
14	$72.50 office delivery		
15			$26 Benny's Deli $95 Chesapeake Cafe
16	$48 farmers' market		
17			
18	$25 deposit Jackson anniversary cake		
19	$93 office delivery		$27 Benny's Deli
20			
21	$89.50 office delivery		
22			$23 Benny's Deli $95 Chesapeake Cafe
23	$195.50 farmers' market		
24			
25			
26	$88 office delivery		$32 Benny's Deli
27			
28	$167.50 office delivery		
29			$87 Benny's Deli $145 Chesapeake Cafe
30	$259.50 farmers' market		
31			
Total	**$1,716.00**		**$729.00**

limit the amount the person can purchase. A young man once came to my farmers' market table and asked if I took checks. He was polite and well-dressed but I got an odd feeling from his demeanor. "Yes," I replied, "but there's a $3 limit." His check eventually bounced.

Warning: Don't ever take starter or counter checks, no matter how good a tearjerker story the person comes up with. Getting a current address and phone number, even with picture identification, does not ensure payment.

If you're selling in a retail street environment, put a little sign on your table and point to it when people ask about checks. If you do take them, let your customers know that you always seek compensation, even if it means using a collection agency or small claims court, regardless of the amount. Just remember, for the most part it's the honest people who will comply with your request or behave in a civil manner. Scoundrels who want your product but have no intention of paying are the ones who become nasty, loud, or teary-eyed. You decide if the product amount is worth the loss of payment. Always remember, it's your business, your money, and your decision. Don't let anyone manipulate you, intimidate you, or push you around.

If you do get a returned check, there are laws that govern the highest amount you can collect. Call or write (using certified mail) and let the customer know that if you do not promptly receive the full amount plus your bank charges, you will proceed with collection. This is often enough to scare some people into paying. Collection agencies, which take a percentage of the recovered costs, are listed in phone directories. If you sell holiday items or gift baskets or anything worth a few dollars, they might accept your work. You may also try pursuing the costs through small claims court if you feel the amount is worth the legal effort and expenses.

2.3 Separating business finances from personal finances

If you are a sole proprietor, I strongly suggest that you keep your business finances separate from your personal finances. This will make the bookkeeping much easier and will help you in understanding what money is *yours* and what belongs to the business. If everything is mixed together, it will be easy to raid your business of funds that you'll need to pay the business bills; or conversely, you'll be able to see if the business can support itself without a constant subsidy.

If you have a partnership, it's imperative that you do not mix your business finances with your personal finances.

3. Hiring a Professional to Help with the Bookkeeping

If bookkeeping seems overwhelming or difficult, a bookkeeper can help you set up the initial work and you can be in charge of filling in the paperwork; a tax preparer can help with filing your taxes.

If, however, you are interested in growing your business and look toward borrowing money from a bank, you will probably need the help of both an accountant and attorney. Otherwise, there are very few times when a home-based food business needs these professional services.

4. Paying Yourself

It's common for many businesses to never pay the owner in the first year or two, and that's fine if you have another source of income. If your spouse, partner, or someone else pays the household expenses, or you have another job, you have time to get your business going. If this is the case, pay yourself sparsely and only when there is excess money that won't be needed for upcoming bills.

If you are responsible for the home bills and must take money for living expenses, you need to be wise with how you do this. Pay yourself a regular salary. Set it at the minimum you need for survival and see if that will keep enough money in the business account to pay the bills. If things get tight with business expenses, try to skip a paycheck.

Cash businesses can be risky for someone with little self-control. Money comes in and it's tempting to spend it immediately. While you need to have a personal income, you also need to build a good base and have money to pay the ongoing business bills.

The food industry is a cyclical business. Depending on your products, especially when preparing for holidays, you might need to purchase a heavy inventory when your weekly income is low. You must look ahead and keep extra money in your business account. Paying on credit can sometimes make life easy; but mostly it can be your enemy.

4.1 Retirement savings

If this is how you are making a living and you have no other source of income, at some point you should consider opening a retirement savings account. It can have tax benefits for your present life while helping you save for the future. Especially if you have no other pension plan, setting up a retirement savings plan is a good idea.

Talk with someone at your bank, an accountant, or a tax preparer. Early in my baking career my brother-in-law, who had been in the insurance business, suggested that I open a retirement account. His persistent suggestions became annoying so I opened one just to keep him quiet. Now I need to send him a thank-you card.

5. Setting up Your Home Office

If you have enough space, set up your bookkeeping so that it's easily accessible, preferably on a desk or tabletop. Keep receipts nearby, and all your necessary work-related office things in one place. This makes it more conducive to regularly doing your books. Bookkeeping doesn't have to take much time, but if you must haul everything out before you begin it can seem like more work than it really is. If you don't have the space, use a box or crate to hold and organize all your papers, and keep the receipts and ledger on top for easy retrieval. You don't have to enter information every day, but designate time at least once a week to do bookkeeping.

Optimally, it helps to get your family used to you working at home so they will allow you the time for business. If they're not supportive, it could be quite detrimental to both your business income and your mental health. Try getting them involved, whether it's by having them package your baked goods, make deliveries, or pick up supplies; participation can help them understand that you are running a business.

Bakery Sugar Cookies

Preheat oven to 375°F and line cookie sheets with foil or parchment.

In a large mixing bowl, cream butter, shortening, and both sugars.

Add corn syrup, vanilla, egg, baking soda, baking powder, and salt. Mix thoroughly.

Mix in the flour, making sure to scrape the dough from the bottom of the bowl. This dough will be very dry.

Drop dough at least 2 inches apart and flatten lightly. Bake for 10 to 15 minutes, depending on size, until light brown around edges.

Cool before storing. Keeps for one week at room temperature or in the freezer for up to six months.

For variations of this recipe see the file on the CD:

Cookies

Yield: 3 dozen large or 8 dozen small cookies

½ cup (1 stick) butter

½ cup vegetable shortening

½ cup packed brown sugar

1½ cups granulated sugar

½ tablespoon corn syrup

1 tablespoon vanilla extract

1 large egg

1 teaspoon baking soda

2 teaspoons baking powder

½ teaspoon salt

3½ cups all-purpose flour

Chapter 6
Purchasing Cooking Equipment, Utensils, and Supplies

This chapter will help you assess the tools and equipment you already have and help you decide what you still may need. It will also give you ideas for where to find the items to stock your kitchen.

1. Cooking Equipment

It's possible to start a business using appliances and tools already in your kitchen. If you're on a strict budget and lack anything, you can borrow or buy secondhand tools and appliances. Items with a few dings or scratches won't look as pretty as new items, but used items can be just as serviceable. Another option is to choose your products based on the available equipment, then as you begin earning money, set some money aside for buying more tools.

If you need heavy-duty equipment such as a processor or mixer, you can find used restaurant and bakery equipment. Look through your local classified newspaper ads under restaurant or commercial equipment, or ask small-business owners for leads. Items can also be found at auctions or through the trade magazines listed in the Resources section on the CD. In addition to these places, used equipment is always for sale on eBay. However, use your common sense when making purchases. Unless you're already familiar with the food business and equipment lines, don't jump into a purchase that might sit in your driveway for two years.

When I started my business I didn't have much money and I lived in an old house with a kitchen that had never been remodeled. The small refrigerator and large but shallow porcelain sink were adequate. I assumed the oven space would not be enough to bake the massive quantities I imagined I would make. I bought a secondhand range, one that had an additional smaller oven on top, for baking cookies, yeast breads, and granolas. My only other purchases were spatulas and a cheap, plastic baby bathtub for hand mixing the large amounts of dough and granola. I didn't even have a handheld mixer. I realized later that the original oven in my kitchen would have handled my production needs, and that an electric mixer would have been a wiser purchase. Friends donated old cookie sheets, I made braided loaves instead of sandwich bread because I didn't have loaf pans, and I traded cookies for a couple of battered tables which I set up in my dining room.

The following sections are an overview of various appliances and equipment. To begin production you won't need most of these but it's good to know about them for when you're ready to increase (or ease) production.

1.1 Worktable and counter space

You must have surfaces for working — whether for mixing batter, rolling dough, cooling pans, or wrapping products. Having enough tabletop or counter work space is very important. If you have counter space but it's currently occupied with miscellaneous stuff, consider reorganizing (remember, less is more), or at least move those items aside whenever you're working.

If you need more work space, set up sturdy folding tables. There are excellent folding tables on wheels you can buy that can be rolled out when you need them and conveniently rolled away when not in use.

Some rolling carts, specifically designed for kitchen use, include a work surface, drawers, and shelving; but any island-type cart, microwave table, or even shelves with wheels can be outfitted to hold your essential work tools. Roll it into the kitchen when you begin and roll it back out when your workday is done.

Kitchen and dining room tables can be protected with large tablecloths or sheets. To further protect surfaces from hot pans, use wire racks, trivets, folded cloths, or invest in a few large cutting boards. I keep three 2' x 3'

wooden boards stacked on the counter next to my oven.

1.2 Refrigerator

When deciding on your product line, think about the amount of refrigerator shelf space you have and maximize it. Your home fridge can be large enough for both family and business needs, especially if you go ahead and consume (or throw out) the food that resides in the back of your fridge.

Cover, date, and label all contents of the fridge. Attach notes as required; once you start production, it's very easy to forget what you have and how old it is. Always rotate your stock. If you really don't have much space, there are small inexpensive refrigerators, but having a second refrigerator is more of a blessing than a necessity. If you want to make pies, cheesecakes, prepared salads, or any foods that require a refrigerator, you may find you do require that second fridge. If you have a large enough production area and a large enough budget, consider purchasing a commercial refrigerator secondhand such as a cooler or a reach-in.

Keep a thermometer inside the refrigerator to be sure it's running 38° F to 44° F (3° C to 7° C). Check it every day.

1.3 Freezers

The freezer compartment in a refrigerator should be used for short-term storage only. To keep ice crystals from forming, the self-defrost function goes into a continual timed thaw and freeze cycle. This has an adverse affect on foods stored for long periods. Every freezer compartment is different, so do shelf-life taste tests to know how long things can last in your freezer before you notice deterioration.

If you have room for a stand-alone freezer and can afford one, this can be a huge benefit. It's invaluable if your venues are mostly holiday or farmers' market outlets where you need to prepare large quantities before the events.

Self-defrost upright freezers are acceptable but manual defrost chest freezers work best. These allow for long-term storage with little deterioration. The annoyance factor of defrosting them once or twice a year is worth the improved quality.

Carefully wrap and store everything. Large, see-through containers are best. Freezer bags are also good but be careful about food breakage. Label and date everything; rotate stock. In addition to freezing baked items, most batters and doughs can also be frozen. When you are ready to use them, thaw them in the refrigerator and stir batters before using. Unbaked yeast dough, however, will only last a week or two before the yeast deteriorates. Remember that every recipe has unique qualities, so you must do product testing before using dough or selling products which have been in the freezer for an extended period.

1.4 Ovens

You don't need a designer or specialty oven. An oven with a simple knob that turns to the desired temperature is just fine. Make sure it has a working thermostat. Gas ovens versus electric is a personal choice; whatever you prefer (or whatever you have at home) will work.

Keep an oven thermometer handy so you know whether or not to adjust the temperature. If your product burns on the bottom from too much bottom heat, make sure the oven is up to the proper temperature before inserting your pans, and use a doubled pan to slow down excess heat.

Convection ovens bake faster, but blow hot air around and can be too hard on the more liquid batters. These ovens can also toughen baked goods and blow muffin tops sideways. If you rent a facility, and all it has is a convection oven, you might need to change or tinker with your recipes. I know how annoying this can be. I once worked in a kitchen with prehistoric facilities. The oven fan was stuck on high and the knob had no temperature markings! If you can't work at home and need to rent a kitchen, inspect the baking equipment and make sure it is what you need to make your products properly.

1.5 Stovetop cooking or frying equipment

If you are going to be doing a lot of frying, keep in mind that some localities regulate stovetop frying or frying equipment. Local fire ordinances might regulate this for the physical safety issue, or health departments may have requirements about the types of fat used and/or how the fat is disposed of or cleaned. Discuss this with your licensing agency. Small countertop fryers might be acceptable, but not commercial equipment; but it depends on your production needs and projected sales.

I used to make delicious whole wheat donuts for the farmers' market using a frying pan on my stovetop, but eventually decided they were too much trouble for too little profit. Frying may end up being too labor-intensive for the purposes of you business.

1.6 Sinks

You must have hot and cold running water and a sink large enough to hold pots and pans, even if you have to tilt your pots to get them clean. *Clean* is the key word.

Your health inspector will make the determination on whether your sinks are up to code or not, but often he or she will bend the rules. For instance, in retail establishments, a small hand sink (designated only for washing hands) or a large mop sink may be required. But the inspector can waive this rule if he or she believes you will maintain a clean environment.

1.7 Cooling rack

A cooling rack (also called a rolling rack or pan rack) is a convenient place to slide your hot trays directly from the oven. These come in varying sizes, from tabletop versions that hold only a few pans to floor models that are carts on wheels. The shorter floor-model cooling rack can double as a work surface. If you have the space, it's an efficient way to cool your baking trays without taking up counter or table space.

1.8 Proof box

A proof box is an enclosed metal box on wheels much like a cooling rack, but with an electric element. It's a warm, moist environment used only for proofing (rising) yeast products. An alternative is to preheat your oven to 150°F to 200°F (66°C to 93°C) then place the dough inside and turn the oven off. You can also be creative and use an empty closet with a heater and pan of water.

If you plan on doing any yeasted products, you should already be familiar with this process. If you're not familiar with it, learn before making any bread plans. Bread making is heartfelt and wonderful, but these products have a short shelf life, are time consuming, and are fraught with problems. If you're not a dedicated bread person, look at other forms of baked goods.

1.9 Microwave

A microwave is not a must-have, but it does make tasks easier. It is handy for little jobs such as heating water, melting chocolate, cooking vegetables, and defrosting. After my early years of not having a microwave, I still find having one a sweet luxury.

1.10 Mixers

If you need a mixer, the handheld types are relatively inexpensive but the motor will burn out so expect to replace one every few months.

If you want to purchase a more convenient stand mixer, look at motor size — the higher the watts the stronger the motor — as well as bowl capacity.

If your business grows and you work with a lot of batters and dough, there are 6- or 7-quart home-style mixers, or commercial countertop models in 10- and 12-quart sizes that can be found secondhand. I now keep a very serviceable 7-quart stand mixer on my counter.

1.11 Food processor

Food processors can often be picked up almost new at neighborhood garage or yard sales but they're not necessary unless you're doing large quantities of chopping or grating. For small amounts of food, the time it takes to clean the food processor can eat up any time you save using it. After the one in my bakery broke, I started hand chopping and found the machine hadn't saved me any time.

1.12 Bread machine

Bread machines don't hold much dough but are perfect if you want to experiment with recipes. You can probably find a decent bread machine at a yard sale.

2. Cooking Utensils and Other Kitchen Necessities

You may have a lot of cooking utensils already, but the following sections may help you decide to buy some additional supplies that will come in handy for your business.

2.1 Saucepans and stockpots

If you'll be doing stovetop cooking, the heavy bottomed saucepans and stockpots keep an even heat and can double as mixing bowls. They often come in sets of graduated sizes and these, too, can be found secondhand. The number you'll need depends on how many products you'll be cooking at the same time.

2.2 Baking sheets, trays, and pans

Most home baking pans are fine for starting a business. Cookie sheets and jelly roll pans don't have to be heavy commercial grade, but the cheapest-quality cookie sheets let too much bottom heat burn your food and can warp at higher temperatures. Double your trays if your oven has too much bottom heat.

I now use jelly roll pans and half sheet trays with one-inch high rolled rims. Some people claim the ridge on these pans interferes with the flow of heat but I've never had a problem. Many restaurants and bakeries also use the full and half sheet trays (with one-inch high rolled rims).

If you have a limited number of baking sheets, consider buying more or asking friends, family, and neighbors for their extras.

For cakes I use the straight-sided shiny aluminum pans that don't stack well, but then the cake sides don't slope, either. Inexpensive muffin and cake pans work well. There are also the flexible silicone pans that are lightweight, inexpensive, and store well, but do need to be placed on a sturdy sheet pan before filling and baking.

Many pans come in nonstick, but regular finish is also fine. Use a pan spray for easy cleanup; or line pans with parchment paper, silicone sheets, Teflon® sheets, or aluminum foil. These need no greasing and your products can cool in the pans. The liners can be used over and over, just wiped down between uses. The exception is aluminum foil, which tears easily. For muffins and sweet breads, consider paper liners, which remain on the products and keep them moister for longer.

There's also disposable, sturdy, paper baking ware and aluminum pans — which are not environmentally friendly and are an added expense — that you bake and sell together with the product so there's far less work and packaging.

Unless it makes you happy, you don't need to purchase expensive, fancy equipment from online sellers, specialty stores, or the home-party type kitchenware companies. Discount and kitchen supply stores always have sales; bakeries and restaurants sometimes advertise their unused pans for sale or auction, and yard sales are always cheap.

2.3 Rolling pins

If you have the strength and will be doing large slabs of croissant, puff pastry, Danish dough, or dense cookie dough such as gingerbread, consider a heavy commercial length (18" or longer) rolling pin. For pies and tarts the lighter rolling pins are good. I now use a wonderful, lightweight, silicone rolling pin.

2.4 Measuring utensils

For convenience, consider purchasing multiple sets of inexpensive spoons and cups for measuring liquids. With extra measuring utensils, you won't have to wash after each messy use. For dry measure, wipe out the utensil with a paper or cloth towel, or hold the cup or spoon upside down over the counter and tap lightly to release any excess ingredients.

2.5 Timers

The most important advice I can share with you is that you should invest in a timer. If you burn something, that's money going up in smoke. Timers with a short ding are okay but the long ring timers are excellent. Whichever one you buy, make sure you use it. Most stoves have built-in timers but the portable ones can go with you as you move around your home.

2.6 Miscellaneous small hand tools

You'll need different sized rubber spatulas for mixing and scraping batters; plastic and metal dough and bench scrapers for cutting dough and cleaning your work surface (hold the flat side against the work surface and push forward); and miscellaneous knives.

Commercial ice cream scoops, the ones with a thumb release, are worth the investment. These are much stronger than the "professional" scoops available everywhere. They come in different sizes for portion control. Once you decide on the best size for your product, using a scoop speeds the process.

A cake or pie marker will place a mark on the top of your products so that each portion is the same size. Wheel markers, sometimes called brownie cutters, mark and cut pans of cakes, bars, and brownies, but this tool can bend and misshape easily. I now use a plastic coated measuring tape and a long, sharp knife.

You'll need decorating tools for decorating cakes, cookies, and other baked goods. There are specialized tools such as straight and offset metal cake spatulas, pastry bags, couplers, tips, tip-cleaning brushes, and flower nails. If you're just starting, you don't need to purchase an expensive decorating kit that contains numerous items you'll never use. Buy a small kit or pick out two or three basic tips and add more when you need it. A turntable is very nice but not essential unless you'll be decorating large, heavy cakes.

For small pans and hand tools, visit flea markets, restaurant equipment supply stores, and the home and kitchen discount stores. There are all kinds of little specialty products available.

2.7 Aprons and towels

There's no law that says you must wear an apron. But they are definitely handy — especially ones with pockets — and useful for keeping your clothes clean and protecting your products against any fallout from your clothes. Aprons also help put you in a working, professional frame of mind. Particularly when you're first starting a business, it's a nice way to begin your day.

Don't forget about towels. A stack of clean dish towels placed near your workstation will be useful for all the unexpected spills and occasional disasters. I prefer hand towels and small bath towels because they are thicker and more absorbent. An old bath towel within reach keeps an oil spill from spreading too far.

2.8 Pan holders and pot holders

Use whatever you feel most comfortable using for pan or pot holders. I prefer long mitts, but some people use dish towels. **Tip:** Keep an aloe plant handy in case you get burned.

2.9 Ingredient scale

If you want a consistent product, the most important use of a scale is for weighing flour instead of measuring by volume. For an accomplished baker working alone, switching to a scale isn't necessary. But if you have problems, or work with an inconsistent baker, consider converting your recipes. Chapter 11 has an ingredient conversion table to help you change volume measures into weight, but it's still important to find out how much your cup of flour weighs.

A scale is also useful for scaling (dividing) dough, and portioning large amounts of batter amongst several pans. For baking small quantities it's possible to simply divide a batter or dough by sight; if your recipe says, "makes two," divide it in half. For larger amounts, weighing the batter gives you a consistent product and more flexibility. Put your pan on the scale, set scale to zero, then pour or scoop batter until the correct weight is reached. (Don't forget to write the pan sizes and corresponding weights on your recipe.)

These scales can be purchased in most restaurant, bakery, and kitchen supply stores.

2.10 Certified scale

If you sell any retail products by weight, such as granola or bread, these must be weighed on a certified scale. Ask your health inspector for specific information, or call your government department of agriculture and markets.

If you sell items by volume or by piece, no scale is necessary. Depending on your local laws, your label should indicate number of pieces or amount.

2.11 Ingredient bins and tubs

Clear tubs are best for storing, stacking, and easily identifying items. If you have floor space, bins on wheels can hold large quantities of sugar, flour, or anything you use in bulk. If these bins are not available, you can place large lidded containers on plant trolleys (caddies) for the same easy access.

2.12 Shelving and racks

Metal and wire racks, the sturdier the better, are cheap, easy to clean, and can be purchased in home improvement and discount stores. Tabletop wire racks for cooling are helpful, but trivets can work just as well.

2.13 Cleaning tools and supplies

Cleanliness will keep you in business. Use the same cleaning supplies you use for ordinary household chores. Bleach is an excellent disinfectant. Add a small amount of bleach to a bowl of water and wipe down all surfaces before you begin working.

If you have small children or animals, vacuum before each work session. While you are working, keep a hand vacuum, broom, or dustpan and brush nearby.

A home bakery will definitely generate more waste than an average-sized family, but not significantly more. A large, lidded trash can should be enough for your kitchen; use your common sense and empty it when necessary.

3. Purchasing Supplies

Equipment and utensils are not the only important things you will need to buy. You will also need to know where to find the best deals on food supplies and packing supplies. This section will help you discover what you may need and where to start your search for your supplies.

3.1 Food supplies

Before you begin buying ingredients for production, shop around your local stores with a calculator, pad, and pen, and record the name of the store and the prices of items you'll need. This way you'll know where to get the best deals. Watch supermarket flyers for weekly specials since there are often huge savings for selected items. The large discount stores have quantity pricing but their items are not always of good quality. You must become familiar with the cost of ingredients and make sure you're comparing ounces to ounces and pounds to pounds (and understand the difference between weight and volume measures). Buy as much as you can reasonably use before it goes out of date, and only if you have enough storage room.

Pay attention to shelf life and storage issues. Quantity is only a good price if you'll use the ingredients before they're out of date. When long shelf-life ingredients such as flour and sugar are on sale, I purchase as much as I can carry. If I find a great deal on nuts or dried fruits, I purchase as much as will fit into my freezer. Remember that you might change one of your existing products so you don't want to get stuck with an ingredient you can't use. If you're on a tight budget, don't tie up your money with extra ingredients, even if something is a good deal.

Buy your ingredients from a reputable business. If flea market items are damaged, you risk using a contaminated ingredient. If they "fell off the back of the truck," you risk possession of stolen goods.

If your business will be generating quantity, find a wholesaler for bulk items so you're not hauling basic ingredients from the supermarket each week. Look for suppliers in the phone book under bakery supply, flour distributor, or restaurant supply.

There's a distinct difference between wholesale stores and the discount stores that cater to retail customers. The wholesale suppliers carry numerous items not available in retail stores and many of their prices are much lower when you buy their quantities and sizes. If you use large quantities of certain ingredients it might be worth buying a case (usually six in a case) of large #10 cans or a pail or full box (average 25 to 30 units) of an ingredient. The price difference between small consumer-sized products and the wholesale versions can be extraordinary. Many suppliers have either online or hard-copy price lists, which make shopping easier. Speak with the sales reps. They're dedicated professionals who can advise and offer suggestions.

Food co-ops and health food stores often give discounts if you buy bulk. Don't be afraid to ask! Purchase an entire bag or box and you should receive a sizeable discount. Sometimes a small local bakery or restaurant will let you order through their supplier, but it depends on their attitude towards perceived "competition."

3.2 Holiday supplies

Seasonal products, both food and paper goods, are often discounted by at least 50 percent by most businesses directly after a holiday. Valentine's products are discounted only because they are covered with hearts, but hearts can be used every day. The July 4th red, white, and blue is patriotic 365 days of the year. Most red or green Christmas products can also be used any time of year.

If you have storage space and are certain that you'll use these items, buy whatever you can manage. The same goes for long shelf-life food products, such as the traditional holiday fruitcake ingredients. Chocolates kept in a cool place also keep a long time.

3.3 Packaging supplies

Most restaurant and bakery suppliers sell packaging as well as ingredients. There are also wholesale commercial paper goods stores (you might need a tax number) listed in your phone directory. Local party supply stores, discount stores, and supermarkets usually sell a limited number of catering and bakery supplies in the most popular sizes, but can often order anything you need (ask about quantity discounts). Be wary of the upscale or specialty places that cater to home bakers and candy makers. Their goods can be very expensive.

The Resources file on the CD lists websites for product and manufacturing companies that can direct you to local suppliers. Sales reps are very personable and knowledgeable, so ask for their suggestions and request samples. I recently needed to purchase ovenable paper bakeware, which are paper baking pans that can simply be filled with batters, baked, wrapped, and sold right in the pan. I wrote the manufacturing company and was sent assorted samples, with a list of suppliers.

Be sure to know what packaging works best before you buy a case. There's often a minimum quantity, but companies might be willing to work with a new business. If in doubt, it may be less expensive in the long run if you purchase smaller quantities and not get stuck with a pallet of, say, eight-ounce glass jars that you eventually learned were too heavy (and needed special handling) for your mail-order cupcakes. What started out as a bargain now takes up valuable storage room.

In addition to food-grade product packaging you'll need outer containers for delivering your goods around town. Recyclable cardboard boxes, plastic milk crates, bread crates, or even paper supermarket bags may work well, but they need to be strong, clean, and neat — remember, you're running a business.

If you're planning on running a mail order business, you'll need outer packing materials in addition to other food-safe packaging. The postal service and private delivery businesses will have products and suggestions. Do a few test mailings to make sure your customers will get their orders in optimal condition. For more information on packaging supplies, see Chapter 7.

Gingerbread Cookies

In a large mixing bowl, cream the softened butter or margarine with the sugar. (Butter tastes better, but the margarine makes an easier dough to roll out. I make these cookies quite often, and use one stick of each.) Add the molasses and egg and beat another two minutes. It may look curdled, but that's okay.

In a separate large bowl, mix the flour, baking soda, spices, and salt. Add to the wet ingredients, mixing on low. Scrape occasionally to make sure all the ingredients are thoroughly incorporated.

When your dough is stiff, separate into two or three disks and wrap well in plastic. Refrigerate for several hours, or for up to two weeks.

When ready to bake, preheat oven to 375°F and line cookie sheets with foil or parchment.

Remove the first disk of dough from the refrigerator. Sprinkle the work surface with flour and place the unwrapped dough on top of the flour. Sprinkle more flour on top of the dough. If you have used only butter and the dough is hard, let it soften for a few minutes.

When the dough feels cold but a finger pressed into the surface leaves an imprint, you are ready to roll. Gently set a rolling pin on top, and start rolling. Occasionally slide a spatula under the dough, or rotate the dough itself. This makes the next step a little easier.

When the dough is about ¼-inch thick, cut the shapes close together and remove to the prepared cookie sheets. Place at least ½-inch apart.

Bake for 10 to 15 minutes, or until they look puffed and a finger pressed gently on top leaves no imprint. For crunchy cookies, bake two or three minutes longer.

Wrapped well, these cookies keep for one month at room temperature, or frozen for up to six months.

For variations of this recipe see the file on the CD:

Cookies

Yield: several dozen cookies (depends on size)

1 cup (2 sticks) butter or margarine

1 cup granulated sugar

²/3 cup molasses

1 large egg

5 scant cups all-purpose flour

³/4 teaspoon baking soda

2 teaspoons ginger

2 teaspoons cinnamon

¹/2 teaspoon cloves

¹/4 teaspoon salt

Chapter 7

How to Name, Package, and Label Your Products

When you have decided what products you will sell, your next step is to consider how you will name, package, and label your products.

1. Product Names

Start thinking about what you'll name your products. A really clever, catchy name can make all the difference to your sales. For example, *Chocolate Cake* is adequate, but *Triple Heaven Fudge Cake* sounds better. My Pumpkin Muffins sold well, but only until I renamed them Country Health Muffins. I had an Apple Cake that was moist and delicious but only reaped average sales; when I renamed it Danish Apple Walnut Cake, sales increased dramatically.

In *Modern Baking* magazine I read about Breadwinner, a Georgia business that started in the home. They began by marketing products called Party at My Place Pumpkin; Better Than a Bubble Bath Mocha Chocolate Chip; and Frankly, My Dear, I Don't Give a Cran. According to the owners, the memorable names reaped numerous mentions in the local press and online bulletin boards, resulting in greater sales.

You certainly don't have to use extreme names, but a simple descriptive name for your product can make its own impact.

2. Packaging

With every product, you must think about how it will be packaged. As you envision different possibilities, consider how each item will move from your kitchen to the customer.

Protection and appearance are top priorities. A good package is economical and keeps your product clean, fresh, and safe from the environment — especially when transporting in different weather situations. The packaging should complement what you are selling and should therefore look attractive and professional — it's part of your advertising, marketing, and professional business appearance.

Packaging can also extend the shelf life of your goods. Put a muffin in a paper bag and it will stay soft and fresh for a day, but use plastic wrap and it can stay soft for two or three days.

If your product has the potential to be greasy or gooey, you will need to consider leakage. Packaging looks terrible when fat oozes through.

2.1 The basics of packaging

As a rule, seeing food through the package can help sales. Remember, people eat with their eyes first. Always think about how your product looks to the shopper.

If you're selling individual cookies from a big tub at the farmers' market, a simple piece of waxed tissue food wrap can work. If the customer wants to take it with him or her, you should provide a bag.

Large cookies, brownies, muffins, or any individual piece of sweet bread or cake can be individually wrapped or placed inside a paper, waxed, poly, or cellophane bag. For wrapping products, use commercial quality plastic wrap (also called cling film or poly wrap).

Whole cakes, loaves, tarts, and pies can be baked in disposable aluminum or ovenable paper bakeware containers.

Find products similar to yours and see how they are packaged. For your products, do a shelf-life package test; make the product, date it, put it away, and go back later to taste test. How long can the products stay like that? For prepared foods, aluminum tins might be convenient for selling items, but they're not for use in the microwave. Styrofoam containers are cheap, but will your coffee cakes begin to taste like the packaging?

Paper and packaging supply companies have salespeople who can help you with any unusual issues. They may also suggest unique ways to make your products stand out.

If you will be seeking wholesale accounts — perhaps you just want to sell cakes to restaurants — you will need cake circles (i.e., cardboard or Styrofoam) and boxes for transporting the cakes. Depending on your agreement with the kitchen manager, you might also need to pre-slice and wrap the cakes in plastic film.

Consider selling a multi-pack product. Instead of a single cookie, sell them by the dozen or half dozen. If you do a variety pack, don't mix flavors unless they are separated within the pack. For example, it's okay to package a vanilla cookie in with a marble cookie (remember to do shelf-life taste testing) but never mix a strong spice cookie with anything else or the entire package will taste like the spice.

Fold-up bakery boxes and the cardboard circles (boards) are used for cakes, pizzas, and any product needing support. Poly bread bags hold cookies, buns, loaves of bread, and anything else that seems appropriate.

If you are selling retail, you'll need paper or waxed bags (I'm partial to white; brown looks too generic) and greaseproof tissue wrap — these are inexpensive and professional in appearance. These items are carried by wholesale commercial paper goods stores such as those listed in your phone directory, and usually have the best prices if you need quantity.

Local party and discount stores sell a limited number of catering and bakery supplies in the most popular sizes, but can often order anything you need. You don't have to purchase by the bundle, and the party store might give a quantity discount if you ask.

Dollar stores are a great resource for miscellaneous items. Specialty stores and online wholesale and retail suppliers have an amazing variety of bags, boxes, and containers that are cute and memorable, but pricey. Decide if the extra cost is worth the kind of business image you want to project.

2.2 Trays and platters

Any solid food can be sold wrapped on a tray. If you're not familiar with trays, do some market research and look carefully at tray and platter construction. Order a tray or two from the local supermarket with the kinds of foods you want to sell. Take them apart to see how they are constructed, then practice creating your own trays.

2.3 Gift packaging, bags, and baskets

Most products, even a loaf of bread or chocolate chip cookies, can be made to look like a gift if wrapped using a special bow or container. Upgrading your products to gifts means they must look especially nice.

Gift packages often give customers the expectation of a longer shelf life, so make sure people know how long each gift will stay fresh.

Gift bags are very easy to create. Use a bag with a handle (colorful paper shopping bags are economical), line it with tissue paper, and place your wrapped products inside. Really, that's all you need! Dollar stores have a good selection and your local craft stores always have sales.

For baskets, any clean basket will work, but you don't have to limit yourself to the traditional basket. Any container that looks nice will do, such as a bowl, colander, box, or anything else that will hold contents. Dollar stores are, again, a great resource. Line the bottom of the container with as much shredded or crumbled paper as you think will make the basket appear full. Select your already wrapped goods and place inside the container until you have a

pleasing look. The more stuffed the basket, the better it will appear. Colorful hard candies, individually wrapped, can add a nice touch when sprinkled over the contents.

To wrap the basket, use special shrink-wrap bags or film, or a stiff Polywrap. Some people don't use wrap and add a bow instead; however, I find the wrap gives it a professional appearance.

2.4 Outer packaging and transporting

When you are considering your product and where it will be sold, also remember that transporting it to the point of sale is your responsibility. Recycled corrugated boxes, commercial plastic bread trays, or milk crates can be used to hold your stacked products. Remember that when you are in public, you are also on display. Your containers should be neat and clean.

Also, if you sell retail at a market or have a delivery route, and the customer purchases several items, it's a courtesy to provide them with a large box or shopping bags.

2.5 Shipping

Mailing your product has different considerations than getting it across town to a farmers' market. You must pack with both the product and customer in mind. Your packaging needs to keep the product fresh. You will also need to consider how others will handle the products, such as the delivery person throwing your box of cookies into his or her delivery van. Your beautifully made cookies may be in pieces by the time they make it to your customer, unless they are packaged in a way to prevent this from happening.

Weather may be a factor in what you can ship; for example, if the product is being shipped in a hot climate, will the items melt?

Consider limiting your products for shipping and keeping fragile or time-sensitive ones for local delivery only. Check with different carriers for their suggestions. Research their reputations and prices. The charges should all be passed on to your customer.

2.6 Eco-friendly

As a businessperson, you must decide how to best wrap your goods. If you are environmentally conscious, you must find a way to satisfy both your political ideals and practical issues. A determining factor for all your product ideas must be how you can get this to the customer in an eye-pleasing, clean, and safe manner. Your target customers might also care about the environment but, consciously or not, they too eat with their eyes first. There are new, environmentally safe products always entering the market, so be sure to ask your supplier for information.

If you are determined to keep packaging to a minimum, consider revolving your business around home eating. You can make food in the customer's container or dish, but this can involve some special issues such as how you collect the dishes and how to make sure that the customer receives his or her own filled dish back.

You can also purchase dishes and have customers leave a refundable deposit. The deposit must be more than the price of the dish so that you can replace the dish if it's broken or not returned. Check with the department that licenses your business to see if they approve of this procedure.

3. Labeling Your Products

Products must, by law, be labeled if they are sold on a self-service shelf or table, where the customer can grab the items. In both the US and Canada, if you provide the service of retrieving and packaging the item, no label is necessary; for example, if you have a table at the farmers' market and help the customers with their purchases, deliver lunch to a building complex, or sell from a coffee cart in an office building, no labels are required. If you are selling your products on a store shelf or anywhere customers can help themselves there must be a label. You also want people to know where they can get more of your wonderful products, so a label is your best advertisement.

All self-service labels must include the following:

- Identifying name of product.

- Net weight ("net" refers to contents only, and does not include weight of package) or number of pieces.

- Name and address of your business (depending on locality, adding the city and state or province might be enough; check with your licensing agency).

- A list of ingredients in descending order of predominance by weight. The ingredient of the largest amount by weight is listed first and so on in descending order.

- Any artificial coloring, flavoring, or preservatives.

- Sell-by date (depending on locality; check with your licensing agency).

Check with your licensing agency for any additional requirements. Sample 7 is an example of a product label.

If there is any variation with ingredient weight from one package to the next — perhaps your bread usually weighs 18 ounces but sometimes a loaf weighs 17 ounces — your label should reflect the lowest possible weight that any package might contain. This way, when there is a variation, you will not be guilty of short-weighing a product. The term "baker's dozen" refers to the 13th-century bakers' practice of including an extra piece, so the baker would not be found guilty of cheating a customer and possibly losing a hand, as was medieval justice.

In general, labels can work to your advantage. They show your product to be professional and legitimate, and provide customers with your contact information so they can order more. Labels can also give other information, such as a web address, reheating or cooking instructions, or anything else that promotes your products. Labels can create good will for your business.

You can create labels with a computer program, have a rubber stamp made (use either a self-inking stamp or a colored ink pad), or purchase custom-made sticky labels that are pressure sensitive.

If you work with a graphic designer and/or print shop to create your labels, always see the proof sheet before your order is printed. Never accept an order if it's less than professional. This also refers to any labels you create on the computer. I've seen sloppy paper labels taped to the bottoms of soggy sweet breads with barely readable smudged ink. Remember, everything you present to the world tells them about how you do business.

3.1 Ingredient list

The ingredient list must include all of the ingredients in your product, by weight, from most abundant to least. (Water is an ingredient!) For example, if the heaviest ingredient in your carrot loaf is whole wheat flour, whole wheat flour should be the first listing. If that recipe only uses a quarter teaspoon of salt, then salt is probably the last on the list. Therefore, you must know the weight of all your ingredients. Chapter 11 has a table of ingredients with both volume and weight measurements.

Be aware about how you designate flour. Such a simple word creates big controversy. White flour comes from the wheat grain and is often listed in commercially prepared products as "wheat flour." While technically true, it's not whole wheat unless the label says "whole wheat." "Enriched flour" or "enriched wheat flour" is white flour, fortified (enriched) with vitamins and minerals to make up for the

SAMPLE 7
PRODUCT LABEL

Blueberry Bumble Muffins

Marcy's Magnificent Muffins — Haymarket, NY

Ingredients: Unbleached flour, sugar, canola oil, berries (blueberries, raspberries, marionberries), orange juice, eggs, cinnamon, baking powder, salt.

Net weight: 6 ounces

---

vitamins and minerals that were taken out during the milling and processing. If you are not sure, just write "flour." All ingredients should be listed by their common name; for instance sugar would be simply "sugar" and not sucrose. See Sample 8.

3.2 Nutrition facts label

In the United States, the nutrition facts label is mandatory only for retail sales (pies and cakes sold to restaurants, for instance, need no nutrition label) and only for businesses grossing more than $500,000. This probably excludes everyone interested in starting a small home-based food business.

In Canada, foods sold at markets, fairs, and roadside stands by the individuals who made them also need no nutrition labeling.

Nutritional facts are not difficult or costly to obtain. You can buy computer software or find a company to research it for a reasonable cost. Also check with your local Department of Agriculture, which may do this as a public service or charge a nominal fee. In the US, the Department of Agriculture has the Cooperative Extension Systems Offices that are staffed by experts that can help you find the information you need.

Depending on the focus of your business and your target market, you might want to include nutritional facts as a courtesy and selling point. For example, if your cookies are healthier than most, or your main outlet is the farmers' market where health and ingredients are part of the customer draw, it might help sales. You can post a sign claiming the products' best feature; for example, "Only 120 calories per cookie" or "Coffee cakes have one serving of fruit per slice."

3.3 Health claims

For all packaging and labels, there are rules about any health benefits you're allowed to claim. Food terms such as light, low, reduced, free, healthy, organic, fresh, natural, and others are key words and/or phrases that are regulated by the government or licensing agency.

For updated labeling requirements in the US and Canada, ask your local health inspector or review information on appropriate websites.

SAMPLE 8
INGREDIENT LABEL

Carrot Loaf — whole wheat flour, soybean oil, honey, carrots, brown sugar, crushed pineapple, eggs, raisins, spices, baking soda, salt.

Chocolate Chip Cookies — unbleached flour, butter, sugar, brown sugar, chocolate chips, eggs, vanilla extract, baking soda, salt.

3.4 Universal Product Code (UPC)

Most small retail stores do not use a fully equipped automated cash register system so the Universal Product Code (UPC) will not be an issue for you. If you want to sell through a large retail chain, you may be asked to supply a UPC. You need to decide if the potential sales of your product is worth the fee, which is usually less than $100 per barcode registration.

To sign up for a UPC number, contact one of the companies listed in the Resources section on the CD. Most midsized outlets, especially ones that take pride in carrying local products, understand the challenges of a small business. Ask if they will simply place their store price tag on your products.

Cappuccino Blondies

Preheat oven to 350°F and grease a 9 x 13 pan.

Combine the instant coffee powder, liquid, and vanilla extract; set aside to cool.

In a medium bowl, combine the melted butter and brown sugar, and then beat in the eggs. Stir in the cooled coffee mixture.

Add the flour, baking powder, and salt, mixing until there are no more lumps of flour. The batter should be cool before adding the chocolate chips or the chocolate will begin to melt and discolor the dough.

Scoop batter into the prepared pan and spread evenly into all the corners. Bake for 30 to 40 minutes, until the blondies are a golden brown and pull away from the sides of the pan.

Cool thoroughly before cutting. Store well-wrapped for up to five days at room temperature, or for up to six months in the freezer.

For variations of this recipe see the file on the CD:

Brownies and Fruit Bars

9 x 13 pan

1 tablespoon
instant coffee powder

1 tablespoon hot water or
coffee liqueur

1 tablespoon vanilla extract

$^3/_4$ cup (1$^1/_2$ sticks) butter or
margarine, melted

1 pound (approx. 2 cups)
brown sugar

2 large eggs

2$^1/_2$ cups all-purpose flour

2 teaspoons baking powder

$^1/_2$ teaspoon salt

1 cup chocolate chips,
semisweet or milk chocolate

Chapter 8
Pricing Products

Your creations are worth something. After all, that is why you are starting your home-based food business! Setting prices can be an overwhelming task, so this chapter will help make the process easier and help you find the worth of your products.

1. Calculating the Costs

There are several ways to price your products. The simplest method is to look at what the current market charges for the same or similar products, then use your best judgment to compare size and quality. Beware of the trap of only looking at price and not quality or uniqueness. Positioning your products to be cheap and competing only on price with supermarkets or novice bakers can be fatal. You don't want to end up paying people to buy your products.

Another easy method is to price by what the market will bear. In upscale or resort areas, prices tend to be higher not only because rents are higher, but because the clientele often don't care about the price.

The most accurate and accepted practice is to know your food costs and charge three to four times the cost of your ingredients, rounding up when necessary. This markup will automatically cover the cost of overhead, packaging, and labor. Use this as a guide and allow yourself some flexibility. For example, if you cost out a muffin with seasonal ingredients and you know that seasonal prices can change from day to day, add a cushion and charge a little extra. This way, your price can remain constant throughout the season. In some venues, it's best to price items so that you can easily make changes. As long as you know your product costs, you can make intelligent decisions.

Here's the formula:

Cost of Product x 3 or x 4 = Price of Product for Consumers

(Remember to round up your answer.)

To find the exact cost per product, you must know the cost of your ingredients, how much the ingredients per recipe cost, and how many pieces you get from each recipe.* Software can be purchased that will ease this process. Software packages vary and come bundled with different tools (i.e., nutritional analysis, cost control measures, sales analysis), so look around to see what works best for you. The Resources section on the CD includes links to recipe software.

For the low tech and least expensive way to figure pricing, you'll need two different kinds of pricing charts: an Ingredient Cost Calculator (see Sample 9) to track all your ingredient costs, and a Recipe Cost Calculator (see Sample 10). This takes initial work but will help you keep track of the cost for every item. For some inexpensive ingredients, such as baking powder and salt, you can simply add a few cents to the final cost. Spices can be very expensive, so they should be carefully calculated.

When your costs go up, you can adjust your prices as needed. With this information at the ready, you'll know how much flexibility there is in varying your price for a specific product. It is important to know if you're making any money on a particular product.

As you can see in Sample 9, if a five-pound bag of flour costs $2.49, one pound of flour costs $0.50. If you look at the ingredient equivalencies table in Chapter 11, you know that there are four cups of flour in one pound. By dividing further you learn that one cup of flour costs $0.13. (On the CD there are worksheets for both the Ingredient Cost Calculator and the Recipe Cost Calculator.) Use this method to complete the worksheets and calculate the cost of all your ingredients. Here's the calculation:

$2.49 divided by 5 lbs = $0.50

$0.50 divided by 4 cups = $0.125

SAMPLE 9
INGREDIENT COST CALCULATOR

Ingredient	Size and Price per Package	Price per Unit	Price per recipe measure
All-purpose flour	5 lbs $2.49	1 lb = .50 4 cups per lb	.13 per cup
Whole wheat pastry flour	5 lbs $3.75	1 lb = .75 4 cups per lb	.19 per cup
Butter	1 lb $2.00	1 lb = 2 cups	$1.00 per cup
Margarine	1 lb .89	1 lb = 2 cups	.45 per cup
Vegetable oil	64 oz 4.99	1 quart $2.50	.63 per cup
Granulated sugar	5 lbs 2.50	1 lb = .50 (2¼ cups)	.22 per cup
Brown sugar	2 lbs $1.59	4½ cups	.35 per cup
Confectioner's sugar	2 lbs $1.59	7 cups	.23 per cup
Eggs	1 dozen $1.69		.14 per egg
Vanilla	16 oz $8.00	32 tbsp or 96 tsp	.25 per tbsp or .08 per tsp
Milk	1 gallon $4.00	1 qt $1.00	.25 per cup
Buttermilk	1 qt $1.59	4 cups	.40 per cup

*For instance, if a 5lb. bag of flour costs $2.50, you must be able to calculate how much of that 5lb. bag goes into your recipe before you can calculate the cost of the product.

RECIPE COST CALCULATOR

Ingredients:
1-2 cups seasonal fruit, chopped
¼ cup oil
¼ cup sugar
1 large egg
1 cup milk
2½ cups whole wheat pastry flour
1 tablespoon baking powder
½ teaspoon salt

Recipe Name: Low-Fat Fresh Fruit Muffins **Yield: 12**

Ingredient	Measure	Cost
Fresh fruit	2 cups blueberries	$2.00 (seasonal price)
Oil	¼ cup	0.16
Sugar	¼ cup	0.06
Egg	1 large	0.14
Milk	1 cup	0.25
Whole wheat pastry flour	2½ cups	0.48
Baking powder	1 tablespoon	
Salt	½ teaspoon	
	Total of ingredients	**$3.09**
	Add a few cents extra for baking powder and salt	0.11
	Total Cost of Recipe	**$3.20**
	Cost of Single Unit	**$0.27 per muffin**

Round up to $0.13 so your answer is $0.13 per cup of flour.

From the above calculations, you can then figure out your recipe cost. As an example, let's cost out the recipe Low-Fat Fresh Fruit Muffins (recipe included on the CD) in Sample 10.

From the recipe cost calculator, you know that each muffin costs $0.27. By multiplying your cost by three or four, you arrive at either $0.81 or $1.08. So you can charge between $0.85 and $1.10 and know that you are making money. However, as stated above, the guidelines can be flexible. If you're at a busy venue and working alone, it might be easier for you to price the muffin at $1.00. But if you know the price of your blueberries fluctuates a lot, charge $1.25 to cover any additional price increases. You're the boss, so with all your information, you can make an informed decision!

Whenever there is an ingredient price change, especially since this recipe uses varying priced fruits, you can easily adjust the price of the muffins and decide if you need to change the retail or wholesale price.

As discussed, the easiest method is to look at similar products on the market. This will let you know what your competitors charge, how your products compare to theirs, and how much consumers are already conditioned to pay. For these reasons I always browse the local grocery stores and bakeries as well as calculating the cost of my products. Since my products are more expensive to make because they're of better quality and a specialty (all natural and healthy, which are not widely available), my prices should be higher. When I find an inferior product that's priced higher than mine, I might adjust my price accordingly.

If you tend to underprice your goods, remember that your time is worth something. Don't price so low that you don't make money. Everyone else makes money from their time and you should, too. Besides, customers who buy from you based solely on price are only looking for a bargain, and they will not be good customers. Those kinds of customers will leave you when the next bargain arrives. You're in business to make money, not donate your labor.

Don't be afraid to put a reasonable price on your goods. Ultimately, there's no point in losing money and most customers do understand. If an ingredient goes up a few pennies, you can probably absorb that price increase, but a large increase or several small ones should make you consider a price or product change.

When I first began, I sold retail through farmers' markets and craft fairs. I consistently used the three-or-four-times pricing system. Unfortunately, there was often another home baker or two at the event, selling their products for far less than mine. Inevitably, they sold out early and then came to my table complaining that they didn't make any money and they weren't going to do this again because it "just wasn't worth it." In the meantime, I'd lost sales from them undercutting my price. At the next event there would be another novice home baker doing the same thing. I learned that these were mostly people who didn't take a professional approach to their business and didn't have a license, so I learned to avoid certain venues that allowed unlicensed food producers.

2. Adjusting for Change in Cost of Goods

The best argument for keeping a current cost-of-ingredients list is that you will always know how much it costs you to make something. Only you can decide if your business will swallow the increase passed on to you from a supplier, or if you must make a price change to continue selling a product. If the price of flour doubles, how much does it impact the cost of one cookie? If the price of pecans triples, what would you do?

Price changes can also be an opportunity to make initial decisions, or later on, revise your offerings. Before setting your price, think about substitutions or changes you can make to the recipe. If, for instance, you make a pecan pie and the price of pecans doubles, you can use a cheaper nut (Winsome Walnut Pie instead of Plain Old Pecan Pie), cut down the amount of nuts (e.g., will the reduction of a quarter cup in a recipe that calls for two cups make a noticeable difference?), or make smaller pies (go from 10-inch to 9-inch tins). You could also offer another relatively low-cost line extension (e.g., Tollhouse pie using walnuts and chocolate chips) and then raise the price of the Plain Old Pecan Pie. This last way, people then have a choice and often do choose the more expensive offering.

3. Wholesale, Retail, and Courtesy Discount Prices

Setting prices can be overwhelming, so once you know how much your product costs and you know what the competition charges, settle on how much you will charge for retail.

Use your retail charge as the base for setting wholesale prices. Wholesale means that the buyer will resell the item and he or she needs to make a profit, too. For most industries, wholesale prices are typically half of the retail price. With perishable foods, however, it can vary from 10 to 25 percent off the retail price; only occasionally is it a bigger discount. For good business relations, only give a wholesale price to a business that intends to resell your products. If you are not sure about someone who requests a wholesale discount, you have the right to ask to see his or her business license or sales tax number.

Retail sales means you are selling directly to the customer. Retail quantity discount is different from a wholesale price. A regular wholesale customer might only need a dozen muffins or one cake, so decide if you will have a minimum purchase for any wholesale account and make that clear when setting up accounts for these type of clients. For my regular account clients, any businesses that picked up their orders could have whatever quantity they asked for.

Delivery was another issue. If the customer was on my route, there was no minimum purchase or delivery charge. If I had to deliver one order, then there was either a minimum purchase or a delivery charge. Of course, you have to work with your account clients and be flexible.

For retail, you can set up a retail quantity discount. Set an amount so your pricing is clear; for example, one item is $1.00 but for six it's $5.90; or if the person buys a dozen they get thirteen (i.e., a baker's dozen); or if they purchase ten, they receive a dozen. You're the boss and you make the decision.

Customers often request or expect a special price because they perceive they are special; since everyone is special, this can create an awkward situation. Plan ahead and establish a courtesy discount policy, which covers your next-door neighbor's cousin, a monthly ladies group with three members, or your child's soccer team coach who really wants a weekly donation. If you believe this person or group should be extended a courtesy, give them something. Your courtesy discount may be a 10 percent discount or a coupon towards a free item if they purchase a certain amount. Schools, civic organizations, and churches can be the most uncomfortable to deal with. This is covered in Chapter 13, section **4.9**, which discusses donations.

If you are going to sell your products both retail and wholesale, the professional approach is to let your wholesale customers know your retail price. Then they can charge the same retail as you do, or price higher, but they will be making an informed decision. You can create ill will by charging retail customers the same as you charge wholesale. Your wholesale customers won't like to find out that you are creating unfair competition and they might not continue doing business with you.

You don't have to decide immediately if you will sell both retail and wholesale and if there will be any minimum quantity for your wholesale customers, but set the pricing so you can be prepared.

4. Wedding Cakes and Other Exceptions to the Rule

There are two major exceptions to the multiply-cost-of-ingredients method:

1. If your product is labor intensive, such as a decorated wedding cake, this rule will not cover your extra labor.

2. If your cost-of-ingredients (e.g., caviar canapés) is extraordinarily high but making the recipe is simple, your pricing might be astronomical using the multiplication method.

With products needing extra labor, keep track of time and charge an hourly rate plus your cost of goods. Add a little more to cover overhead. See what competitors are charging and make adjustments.

Most wedding cake prices are figured by the slice, so calculate your costs and add labor, then divide that amount by the number of servings. This pricing structure could also be used for any specialty cake requiring a great amount of detail work.

Conversely, if your recipe involves a typical amount of labor but your ingredients are unusually expensive, you could still use the cost-of-ingredients method but consider reducing your charge so that it's customer-friendly. Deduct any amount that seems reasonable, or try pricing at two times the ingredient cost. Do whatever seems fair.

4.1 Contracts for wedding cakes and other special orders

It's helpful to have a contract for any special orders (especially wedding cakes). Sometimes a dispute is as simple as a misunderstanding, or forgetfulness when it comes to payment.

As a business owner you can write a simple contract and ask a customer to sign it. A contract defines the agreement, helps with misunderstandings and memory issues, and can be used in court if you have a problem.

The contract should include the parties' names, dates, special details, price, and additional comments. Both parties should sign the agreement and each keep a copy. See Sample 11 for an example of a contract. The CD includes a blank Wedding Cake Contract for your use. The blank contract can be adapted for any special orders.

WEDDING CAKE CONTRACT

A Piece of Cake!
555-555-5555
14 Pedestal Lane, Anywhere 99405
Patty Cake, owner

Order date: September 10, 20--
Wedding date: August 15, 20--
Client's name: Maxine Trumpet
Phone: 555-555-6555

Number of servings: 200
Cost per serving: $4.50
Total: $900

Set up time: 10 a.m.
Delivery or pick-up: Delivery, $45 additional charge

Event location and phone: The Arbor House 555-555-8888
Contact person at location: John Arbor, owner; Nancy Poplar, manager

Cake Details

Cake flavor: Carrot cake
Cake filling: Vanilla buttercream
Cake frosting: Vanilla buttercream
Flower details: Fresh flowers
Main color: Orange
Accent color: Yellow

Number of tiers: Four sizes of tiers — 6, 10, 14, 18

Comments:
 Flowers to be provided by bride and delivered by florist to Arbor House the day before
 the wedding.

Deposit: $50 paid September 10, 20--.
Balance due: Two weeks before event $895 ($900 cake + $45 delivery – $50 deposit)

I have read and understood the above and have received a copy for my records.

Maxine Trumpet   Date: September 10, 20--
Client's Signature

Patty Cake   Date: September 10, 20--
Owner's Signature

Chocolate Overdose Brownies

Preheat oven to 350°F and line a 9 x 13 x 2 pan with foil or parchment paper. This recipe makes a lot of batter so make sure your pan is high enough. (Alternatively, use two 8-inch or two 9-inch square pans.)

Melt the unsweetened and semisweet chocolates with the butter. Cool for ten minutes.

Mix in both sugars, beat in the eggs and vanilla, then the flour, baking powder, and salt.

Scoop about half of the batter into the bottom of each lined pan, and spread to the edges. Then take your candy bars and line up close together, covering the batter. Some gaps are okay.

Carefully scoop the remaining batter over the chocolate and again spread to cover, smoothing the batter to cover the chocolate candy bars. For the larger pan size, bake for 45 minutes then reduce heat to 325°F and bake 15 minutes longer. If the brownies still seem soft and wet when a toothpick is inserted near the center, turn the heat down to 300°F and bake for another 15 minutes. This should be enough time to thoroughly bake the batter. For smaller pans, adjust the time.

Cool thoroughly before cutting. Store well-wrapped for up to five days at room temperature, or for up to six months in the freezer.

For variations of this recipe see the file on the CD:

Brownies and Fruit Bars

9 x 13 x 2 pan

1 package (8 ounces) unsweetened chocolate

1/2 cup (3 ounces) semisweet chocolate

2 cups (4 sticks) butter

2 cups brown sugar

1 1/2 cups granulated sugar

6 large eggs

2 tablespoons vanilla extract

2 1/4 cups all purpose flour

1 1/2 teaspoons baking powder

1 teaspoon salt

Approximately 1 pound of your favorite chocolate bars

Chapter 9
Where to Find Your Customers

Your business can be a combination of wholesale and retail. Wholesale is where you sell to a business, which will then resell your products to the consumer. Retail is where you sell directly to the consumer. Your choice of products will determine the best sales options.

If you're still undecided about what products to make, read through this chapter and see what venues feel most comfortable for your skill and lifestyle. Match your product with the market you're interested in servicing. Think about your product choices and where they would do the best. For instance, granola might sell well at a farmers' market, but not in a convenience store. Individual pieces of streusel-topped coffee cake might sell when stacked on the counter at that same convenience store, but not on the shelf in a supermarket. Slices of cake and pie might be a great fit for the dinner menu in a sit-down restaurant, which brings up another point. When you are selling desserts to restaurants you will need to consider how or if the dessert will be promoted. For example, if the restaurant trains its servers to promote dessert, or there is a dessert tray sent to each table, your cake or pie will sell well.

As you make decisions, you need to look at the not-so-obvious. Think about the *convenience* factor and be realistic. If one venue doesn't work, try another. Most baked goods are considered impulse purchases. Just because your food is delicious doesn't mean that someone will travel across town to buy it. Think of how you can get your foods conveniently to the customer.

1. Wholesale: Finding Businesses that Will Sell Your Products

The first step in finding wholesale customers is to identify businesses that sell your type of product. You may want to consider beginning your search in the following areas:

- Convenience stores

- Natural foods stores

- Neighborhood markets and midsized supermarkets

- Specialty or gourmet stores

- Restaurants, diners, delis, and coffee shops
- Bookstores
- Via caterers and party planners
- Through online merchants

Ask others, such as friends or acquaintances, if they know of any places where your products might fit. Do you want to offer a finder's fee? A dozen cookies or muffins can be great incentive. My best ever account came from a tip. "I was up on campus last week," said one of my secret agents, eating a warm triple chocolate chip cookie. "I passed a little snack area run by students and there was a line down the hallway." Their lines got longer once they began selling goods from my bakery. The student manager, whom I called immediately, was easy to work with and the account grew to six-dozen muffins and five-dozen cookies daily, Monday through Friday. That's a lot to churn out from a home kitchen.

Whether you visit or phone, always ask for the manager or owner, and always be respectful of the person's busiest times. In other words, never call or visit a restaurant just before or during mealtime when it is busy with production or serving meals. Optimally, you would call and make an appointment. Ask when it's convenient for the person, mention that you will only take five minutes since you know he or she is busy, and say that you will bring samples of your products. Business people rarely turn down free samples. If you're nervous or get tongue-tied, write up a brief outline before calling. My first year I kept a full script beside the phone so I wouldn't forget my name or why I was calling!

For this entire process, you will need enthusiasm, confidence, and thick skin. With each business you approach, hope for the best but understand that you won't always succeed. Arrive on time in business-casual attire. In 25 words or less, introduce yourself and say why you have something the person's customers want that no one else has. Show your price list and samples. Remember, everyone eats with their eyes first and their stomachs second; nothing will sell your business more than professional-looking and delicious-tasting samples.

Project competence and cheerfulness. Always look and act in a professional manner. This means clean clothes and no nasty words about your competition. Smile and show your excitement and expertise in creating consistent, delicious foods.

Not every business will be interested. Remain cheerful, say "thank you for your time," and don't let it discourage you from continuing to look for other outlets. If you've never done "cold calling" before, it can seem daunting. The more you do it, the more you will learn, and the better you will get. If the person does express interest, be prepared to answer questions about delivery, minimum orders, billing, and extending credit. Be clear on your standards; set minimum orders, financial terms, and geographic boundaries. It's okay to be flexible when you're first starting, but remember that you are in business to make money. Have a notepad and pen and if you don't know the answers, make yourself a note and ask for the best way to contact the person.

I strongly suggest starting all wholesale accounts on cash on delivery (COD). Don't let people intimidate or pressure you for credit. Food businesses have the highest failure rate amongst all businesses and it's very easy for them to hide financial problems from suppliers. The greatest outlet that doesn't pay its bill is worse than not having an outlet. Look at all the money, effort, and time you spent with nothing in return.

1.1 Restaurants, diners, delis, and coffee shops

If you have an excellent cake or pie recipe, local eateries are great outlets. Forget the national chain restaurants because they don't usually stray from company standards. The smaller regional and local restaurant owners and chefs, however, understand the appeal in having made-from-scratch desserts. Sometimes these eateries have a pastry chef on staff, but more often they purchase factory desserts from their suppliers or have a simple selection of slap-together menu items, such as ice cream sundaes or brownies à la mode.

Several times I've been delighted when an owner or chef has listened to my (prepared) monologue, tasted the samples I brought, and then asked if I could provide him or her with a signature dessert. If this happens to you, simply tweak one of your best recipes and remember that you cannot sell "their" dessert to any other business. If you have a cake or pie recipe that people rave about, this is a good place to start. Think about presentation and consider whether your specialty dessert needs to be spruced up. Maybe add a buttercream border, some nuts around the sides, portion markings on top (mark these with a knife), or use little candy pieces to show the number of cuts in each cake. Be prepared to discuss creating a dessert specifically for them, and remember it will be a signature item that is available only in that one restaurant.

In addition to selling desserts from a menu or a pastry or dessert cart, there might also be room in the lobby of a restaurant or near the cash register to display your homemade goods. Sometimes a restaurant will sell pre-boxed coffee cakes and breakfast pastries on Friday and Saturday evenings. Jams and preserves made from local produce can be a natural fit in resort areas. Holiday items such as cookie trays, gift baskets, or specialty cakes and breads can be sold to patrons on their way home.

Think about how you will make and transport your desserts to the restaurant. Pies can be baked in aluminum foil pans and cakes can be placed onto disposable cardboard circles. For delivery you will also need fold-up bakery boxes, which come in all sizes, but always use taller boxes that leave a couple inches of clearance. That extra space inside ensures the cake or pie arrives in perfect condition. These supplies can be purchased at party stores or in bulk from paper goods suppliers. For the budget-minded person, cutting out circles from cardboard cartons might seem like a good idea, but if you bake more than two cakes a week, it will become quite annoying.

If you are approaching an alternative type eatery that encourages recycling, use your dinner plates and let them know that the enviroment is an issue for you. They will love that you've thought about it and perhaps they can start you off with a few of their plates.

1.2 Stores and markets

Stores and markets will often sell home-baked goods individually wrapped or in packs of 6 or 12. Occasionally a market will sell small, whole cakes or pies. If the manager of a market is interested, determine delivery days by shelf life and sales turnover.

Be wary of consignment or buy-backs: In other words, be careful about taking returns on what is not sold. Any damage the store or customers do to your goods becomes your loss. Large wholesale bread companies often do this, but reputable stores rarely ask a small business to take the loss. Remember that if you decide to take returns, don't sell them for a reduced price or give them away. Get rid of them. Once the products are out of your control, anything could have happened to them, such as contamination. For example, maybe one of the store's customers opened the wrapping on your muffin but decided not to purchase it. That customer might not have washed his or her hands in several days! Or maybe an employee opened your fudge, took a bite off the end, smoothed it over with a finger, and wrapped it back up. For your own protection, you should throw away any returns.

1.3 Caterers and party planners

Businesses that specialize in catering or event planning will often buy bread products and desserts rather than spend the time making their own. Price is not as much of a concern since they often pass the costs on to their customers.

1.4 Online merchants and catalogs

Have you seen some of the upscale food catalogs and websites? Their goods are quite expensive — one catalog sold nine fancy cupcakes for $59 — and many of these companies buy from small businesses. If you have an unusual product, something that sets you apart, solicit these regional or national companies.

Create a professional letter, include full-color pictures of your product, and send out several queries along with samples. Stress the homemade, small-batch quality and you might get a positive reply.

Here's the catch: If the company likes your product, you must be able to provide the quantity it needs and have enough capital to purchase the required ingredients. Then you have to wait for payment until 30 days after the company receives your goods. That can become very expensive. You will need a contract from them, and make sure your attorney reviews it before you start production.

See the Resources section on the CD for links to wholesale and retail mail-order outlets.

1.5 Florists, gift shops, and specialty boutiques

These businesses generally do not purchase foods for resale, but they are in a great position for recommending your services. Call ahead to make sure the manager will be on-site, then bring a sample plate and business cards. Let the manager know that you, too, are in the business of recommending other businesses to *your* customers.

2. Retail: Finding Your Customers

You already have a potential retail customer base if you work outside your home, attend classes, or are otherwise active in the community. Selling to the people you come into contact with is a great place to start.

If you have already been giving your goods away, it can be hard to get those people to begin paying for products you used to give away for free. If this is the case, and you feel uncomfortable, sell items that you have not previously given away — perhaps tweak a recipe so it appears to be different. Don't be shy and don't let moochers manipulate you into more freebies.

Create a flyer to announce your new business and list the items you're selling along with size, price, and any interesting details. Tell everyone you meet about your business and give each person a flyer.

2.1 Street fairs and markets

There are local farmers' markets, flea markets, street fairs, crafts fairs, church and school bazaars, and assorted special events where food vendors are welcomed. To get a booth at a crafts fair or farmers' market, either call or visit these locations and ask for the manager. Explain who you are, what you would like to sell, and ask about becoming a vendor. The manager or organizer will take it from there.

For other retail sales outlets, keep an eye on your local community bulletins or newspaper for listings under "calendar" or "special events" and call for information. A food handler's license is often required, and your locality might also tax prepared foods. Call your local tax authority for rules.

Each venue is different, so ask yourself the following questions:

- Is the potential profit adequate to counter the vendor charge? This depends on the expected crowds; the more foot traffic, the better your chances of making money.

- Is the venue out in the open or inside? Weather-dependent venues are risky unless you have a covered booth.

- Is your food appropriate for the time of year? For example, lemonade, cookies, cupcakes, and ice cream are great for summer days, but not so great for winter fairs.

- How far is it from your home? Hauling food across town is a lot different from driving three or four hours. As a rule, it's not usually worth time and travel expenses to participate in an out-of-town venue unless you can charge a little more to cover the additional travel expenses, or you sell high-profit items.

- Are you selling impulse foods to be eaten on the spot, or gifts and prepackaged mixes hoping customers will take them home? People are always hungry; but prepackaged items are best for holiday sales.

Every venue needs individual evaluation. For instance, some flea markets might draw people only wanting to get a great bargain on socks, while others might cater to high-end hungry folks with plenty of money for food. A holiday school bazaar with 20 crafters will not bring in the same crowds as a holiday craft fair held at the county fairgrounds.

Having a lot of competition shouldn't be a deciding factor. I recently attended a busy regional farm market in upstate New York. It was winter and very cold. Most shoppers were buying potatoes, apples, hot coffee, and dollar bargains. I passed numerous tables of homemade cakes, breads, and cookies, most of which were inexpensive and (unfortunately) many appeared sloppy and unappetizing. These vendors had very little business. The only really busy homemade food booth was run by a well-polished young man wearing a crisp cranberry apron. His table was presented in an upscale mode with an ironed cranberry tablecloth, several sterling silver pedestal cake stands of differing heights, and a large professional sign set solidly on the table. He was selling dried fruits and potato chips dipped in chocolate. These were packaged in delicate looking poly bags and little decorated boxes. The expensive dipped delights looked cute and yummy. He had a line of customers. Appearances are very important and should not be overlooked.

2.1a Setting up a retail table display

You can learn a lot from setting up a booth for a few weeks. If you decide to try a booth-style venue, start small and simple. Find out the following details:

- Who will supply the table?

- Where can you unload your products and park?

- What are the set-up and take-down times?

- What other types of food vendors will be there?

- Do the organizers offer any relief for taking breaks? Some street fairs have volunteers who will watch your booth; otherwise, bring a partner or hope a friendly vendor beside you will watch your booth while you use the facilities.

Your table should be neat and clean. Use tablecloths or fabric (flat sheets are excellent) and try covering the table completely to hide the legs and any storage area underneath. Making it look particularly nice is an advantage — it may make it stand out more, thus attracting more customers. Add doilies, pedestal cake stands, baskets lined with cloth, and mirror trays. Use bright color combinations and props such as wooden mixing spoons or measuring cups, which give nonverbal cues that everything is made from scratch. Bring business cards, flyers, or other promotional materials, and encourage people to take them.

Be professional. Make sure your goods are fresh; for example, bake cookies and muffins the afternoon before, but make sandwiches that morning. Have signs for your products with names and prices — even handwritten signs are good. Customers like to know what they are looking at and how much the items cost. If things are not labeled, many potential customers will simply walk by without asking. After a short while, those who do ask will begin to annoy you. Save everyone a lot of grief — use labels.

A basic rule for product display: *The more you have, the more you sell.* An overflowing basket of muffins looks appealing. A sparse display appears drab and lifeless. Psychologically, shoppers are drawn to a table that screams *abundance*. Use this rule as a guide. If it's the

end of the day, shoppers don't expect a full supply, but in the first few hours, make your table look plentiful. If, for whatever reason, you don't have too much sitting out, try other tricks such as using smaller plates or baskets, which makes your display appear to have more product than it does; using shredded paper or styrofoam packing as filler and then putting your wrapped food on top; or lining a deep basket with wadded paper, covering it with a cloth, and displaying your foods on top.

Be sure to have enough spare change for the entire day. Use a secured box, deep apron pockets, or a special money or change bag to keep your money safe. Write down how much money you start with and deduct it from the amount at the end of the day. That's how much you made. It's easy to make mistakes or get confused, so pay attention to this part. How much money you earn is the entire reason for your being there.

Accepting cash is always best. Checks are dangerous unless you know the check-writer very well. Even then it can be a problem. Never take "counter checks" which have no printed name and address on them. Avoid starter checks. If you feel uncomfortable, apologize and explain that you don't take checks. Taking credit cards can be a real hassle if your products are only a couple of dollars (but worth the bank charge if you sell large items or provide mail order). You can also direct your customers to the closest ATM. See more about this very important topic in Chapter 5, section **2.2a**.

Every item you sell should be prewrapped or handed to the customer using either a piece of food grade wrap or a disposable glove. Bring enough bags — customers like getting a bag, even if it's for one cookie that they will immediately eat. Use boxes if your baked goods are delicate or gooey. Boxes look very nice with a doily on the bottom. It's not eco-friendly, but it docs look nice. I've seen table displays with bakery boxes propped open and the boxes filled with a few products. This is a wonderful visual cue for shoppers and subtly suggests how they can take their purchases home.

Think about any products that might go along with your homemade goods. If you sell cookies on a hot day, homemade lemonade or cans of soda can be extra revenue. If it's a chilly autumn farmers' market, think about hot drinks or a slow cooker filled with chili to accompany your breads. To avoid getting stuck with any unsold add-ons, only purchase (or make) items that have a long shelf life or that you and your family could consume if not sold.

Including samples on your table is up to you — it can depend on the kind of products you sell, the area where you live, and your personality. Having a little tray of samples can encourage sales, but can also be viewed by the public as nothing more than free food. Having cut up cakes and cookie pieces mounded on a platter invites repeat grabs from people with no intentions of buying anything. They believe it is their right to eat whatever is put onto that plate and then move on when they're full. If you decide to provide samples, consider placing a small amount in sample-size cups. Many stores use this method. It keeps the food sanitary and limits the amount that most people will take, so it helps to stop freeloaders.

Allow time to set up and break down your display. Make a list of what you will need to bring and check it off as you are packing (see Sample 12). Be prepared for changing weather and bring a comfortable folding chair; working a venue can make for a long, tiring day. Have a cooler with drinks and substantial food for yourself; bring a thermos with something hot if it's cooler weather. Bring an extra sweater or jacket, and an extra clean shirt.

On the CD there is a Retail Market Venue Supply Checklist for your use.

2.2 Mobile carts

If you're selling food from a cart on the street, there are requirements for meeting mobile vendor health codes (i.e., sanitation and refrigeration). You'll need a special permit in addition to your production license. Call your local municipality for details.

A mobile cart venue could be lucrative, or more trouble than it's worth. Many years ago I sold cookies, wholesale, to two enterprising young men who had just arrived from another state. They outfitted an old-fashioned Model-T car into a sales venue and did great business on the university campus until wintertime. I never saw them again so hopefully they just moved their business to a warmer climate. Thankfully, I'd just instituted a COD-only for all accounts, with no exceptions, so they didn't owe me money when they disappeared.

2.3 Office delivery route

Consider setting up a delivery route where people can order ahead and/or purchase from a daily selection. Decide on a time frame and products (e.g., breakfast foods, snacks, box or bag lunches). Then create a simple flyer with prices and graphics using line drawings, a border, and colors to make the flyer more attractive. Take the flyer to a few area offices — preferably with food samples for any hesitant decision makers.

The flyer in Sample 13 encourages anticipation of the business owners' arrival with food on a cart or in a basket, which makes for greater sales.

Office complexes, schools, banks, hospitals, and anywhere there are numerous hungry people are all potential markets. If you know

RETAIL MARKET VENUE SUPPLY CHECKLIST

When you pack to leave for the event, check off each item as you load the vehicle.

Display
- ☐ Table and table coverings
- ☐ Additional display items (e.g., doilies, props)
- ☐ Product signs, product labels
- ☐ Price signs
- ☐ Policy sign for accepting cash, checks, credit cards, and debit cards
- ☐ Paper, marking pens, tape, scissors

Products
- ☐ Triple Berry Muffins
- ☐ Banana Bran Muffins
- ☐ Sugar Cookies
- ☐ Chocolate Chip Cookies
- ☐ Veggie Wraps
- ☐ Iced Tea

Sales
- ☐ Copy of license and sales permit
- ☐ Extra change (bills and coins)
- ☐ Credit and debit card machine (if using)
- ☐ Receipt pad
- ☐ Calculator

Miscellaneous
- ☐ Disposable gloves
- ☐ Aprons
- ☐ Waxed tissue wrap
- ☐ Plastic wrap
- ☐ Cups and spoons
- ☐ Paper bags
- ☐ Plastic bags
- ☐ Bakery boxes
- ☐ Knife or serving utensils

Miscellaneous Supplies
- ☐ Tissues, towels, paper towels, and cloths
- ☐ Garbage bags
- ☐ Tub of bleach water
- ☐ Small broom and dustpan

Personal Comfort
- ☐ Extra clothing
- ☐ Cooler with drinks and food
- ☐ Chair
- ☐ Cell phone

Margie's

Baked Daily

Call for daily selection:

Bag Lunch
Sandwich of the Day, chips, cookies, $4.95 each

Boxed Lunch
Sandwich of the Day, chips, pickle, salad, cookies, soda, $7.50 each

DROP COOKIES $1.50 each
Chocolate Chip • Peanut Butter • Gingersnap
Oatmeal Raisin • Snickerdoodle • Chocolate Midnight

Party Platters Available
with 24-Hour Notice

DELIVERING TO THE CENTRAL CITY BUSINESS DISTRICT M-F

Our products sold at all SuperDeli locations,
the Saturday downtown Farmers' Market, and by calling us:

Marge and Ernie 555-555-5555
Free Delivery within city limits

someone who works in any of these places, he or she can provide an ideal introduction. Ask at your bank or credit union, and let them know you are one of their customers. Make a list of businesses in adjacent locations and call the owners or managers to see if this is allowed.

Think about how you will describe yourself; for example, as a coffee-cart service, lunch cart, or lunch-basket business. Prepare your script: "Hello, I'm Margie Vendor, I own a licensed business. I make delicious homemade sandwiches and cookies and I'm interested in selling my goods at your place of business."

Office buildings in larger cities often have an arrangement with on-premise coffee shops or restaurants that prohibits outside vendors; and some buildings have an exclusive contract with coffee-cart services. However, there are many office buildings and complexes that don't have a formal agreement and might welcome your delivery service.

If you get a negative response from the building's management office and they won't allow you to solicit, it's possible to target individual businesses within the building by asking permission from an office manager or business owner. (Remember that samples of your product can be persuasive.) You won't have the freedom to visit all of the offices, but you're allowed to go where you're invited. It's important to get permission; otherwise, you are trespassing. You only need a small number of businesses to make this work. Beginning small scale can eventually lead to a thriving business with a good customer base.

2.4 Wedding cakes and other specialty products

For anyone who bakes and/or decorates delicious, spectacular cakes, the specialty cake business is a perfect fit. You need business cards and a flyer that emphasizes why your products are special — the taste, the visual, or both! My wedding cakes were visually modest, always decorated with real flowers, but each tier had a different all-natural and made-from-scratch flavor.

It can take years to build a wedding-cake-only business, but branching out into other special and all-occasion cakes can keep you in steady production while building your reputation. Think about selling wholesale to upscale restaurants, and retail at upscale markets or craft fairs. (For your more expensive specialty items, bazaars and flea markets will not be worthwhile.) Pass out flyers and donate cakes to community events; always leave a few business cards nearby.

If family, friends, coworkers, and neighbors have already designated you the cake person (who donates for each occasion), let them know you are officially in business and thank them for all their help and support. Give them a few flyers to hand out. If you are kind and generous, some folks may qualify for the courtesy discount. If you are too uncomfortable to ask for cash, bartering is always a nice option. Just remember that you are in business now and it's okay to charge for your skilled services; or at least have a reciprocal arrangement. Other professionals make money for their time and services, and you should, too.

2.5 Residential neighborhood sales

Neighborhoods near your home might be a suitable and convenient source of business, especially if you offer home-cooked meal items and/or special home-baked desserts. Neighbors working full time may appreciate home-cooked meals delivered hot to their doors, or in microwaveable containers with reheating instructions.

Make flyers and take them to residential developments or apartment buildings (see Sample 14). These flyers should have a sentence or two about your business, a descriptive list of your products and prices, the ordering and delivery process, and any minimum order and/or delivery fee. If you're uncomfortable giving out flyers in neighborhoods, an alternative is to mail postcards.

2.6 Kitchen sales

Kitchen sales is a version of neighborhood sales. If you feel at ease with the idea of having strangers come into your living space, you could sell from your kitchen. This might work best if you live in a large apartment building, condo complex, or self-contained neighborhood development.

Send out flyers and ask customers to place orders for pick-up. It's important, however, to make sure your licensing allows for this, and to post limited retail hours or you might have people stopping by when you're not in business mode.

2.7 Mail order

The world is your marketplace when you set up a website or use online store sites and Internet malls to sell your products. Looks easy? Remember that things are not always what they seem. Practical issues such as freshness, handling, packaging, and product returns must be given serious consideration. Be realistic about potential sales and think about the headaches involved. Visit online businesses (some are listed in the Resources section on the CD) and look at their products, pricing, packaging, and ordering guidelines.

Check with your local licensing agency if you plan on shipping any products. Some areas have rules and regulations that apply to the shipping of specific items.

Do a search to see how many similar products are already available. Specialty items — those not available to consumers in their own area, or items so totally unique that they cannot be copied by your competitors — have the best chance for sales. This book will help you select, make, and package products, but for specific help with running a mail-order business, see the listings in the Resources section on the CD.

2.8 Holiday sales

Everyone becomes a potential customer; even people who don't usually care about baked goods are intent on presenting the best to their family, friends, neighbors, and coworkers. Many businesses send gifts to their clients and purchase food for holiday parties; many people who work don't have the time or inclination to make their own homemade foods.

Gift baskets, gift bags, and cookie trays can be sold to corporations that send out a substantial number of client gifts. Banks, law firms, and accounting agencies have been my best customers. I make gorgeous cookie trays and baskets for my customers to send to their clients. I have had to limit the number of orders each year because each customer would typically order a dozen or so at once.

To solicit business, the Chamber of Commerce has a list of businesses that like to participate. Call the business or office manager of local medical, insurance, marketing, public relations, advertising, or realty companies. Also try the purchasing agents for factories and manufacturing plants.

Most of the larger companies place orders several months in advance, so make your calls early. Find out if there is any interest in your product and get the name of the person who does the buying. Put together a nice flyer or brochure (see Sample 14) or write a brief cover

Hello Neighbor! Have you heard about us?

Green Bean & Biscuit

Home Meals and Bakery

We know how hard it is to come home from work after a long day and make a delicious, nutritious, cost-conscious meal. But now you have us! We live in your community, prepare our foods in a licensed kitchen, use many local products, and we deliver!

Real homemade food right to your door and at your convenience.

Call for more information:
555-555-5555

Dinner Options

Tempting.Weekly Specials   Soup of the Week   Hot Dinner Specials

This week:

Fresh Salads: Greek, Grilled Chicken Caesar, Asian Tofu
Main course: Pasta with vegetables, Meatloaf, Chicken with sautéed broccoli

Additional Options

Fresh Baked Breads   Buttermilk Biscuits   Cinnamon Rolls

Vegetable Rolls (local produce only!)   Whole Grain Muffins

Weekend Entertaining

In addition to our weekly menus we have

Delicious Deli Sandwiches and Platters   Meat & Cheese Platters

Dessert Options

Homemade Cookies   Homemade Cakes   Specialty Desserts

Mention this flyer and receive a side order of our locally grown green beans and scratch biscuits for four with your first dinner order.

SELF-COUNSEL PRESS — START & RUN A HOME-BASED FOOD BUSINESS 09

letter. For example, "A homemade product is more personalized than a commercially produced item," or, "A delicious homemade gift expresses a warm, thoughtful feeling in a season of holiday and family cheer." Remember to offer samples.

Smaller local businesses probably won't approach corporations until they are well-established. Network — if you know people who work in these businesses, call and let them know you are in business and ask who's in charge of holiday gifting. In September or October, drop off or mail your flyer with a sample.

You will need a special flyer for the holidays to promote your homemade goodness. See Sample 15.

For an example of a holiday letter, see Sample 16. The holiday letter should be addressed directly to the potential customer. End the letter by saying you will call the person within one or two weeks. It is important that you follow up. One or two positive responses could put you into steady production.

Additionally, packaged food items, such as gift baskets and trays that are completely wrapped, might find a special venue for the holiday season. If the food product is wrapped and not left in the open, local retail laws might allow nonfood establishments such as clothing stores, gift and card shops, and jewelry shops to sell holiday foods.

2.9 Celebrating year-round

The holidays used to refer to December festivities, but now any holiday is an occasion to celebrate. Try promoting cookie trays, gift bags, and gift baskets for special occasions or public holidays. You can adapt products to these events by simply changing the packaging, colors, or shapes.

Flyers and advertising can then be created to move from one special occasion to the next.

Realtors often send gift certificates to new home buyers. This would be a unique way for the real estate company to say, "Welcome to the neighborhood!" while introducing the new homeowner to a local business. Several agents regularly ordered my trays with cut-out cookies featuring shapes of houses, pets, and people.

2.10 The custom gift business

Corporate gift-giving is a huge, year-round business. In slow economic times, there can be more of an incentive for a company to save money by using you, a local source, for these gifts. This knowledge can be used in your strategy.

Many companies regularly send gifts to their clients and employees, often using imprinted promotional products. For many years, coffee mugs and t-shirts were the norm, but you can gain a dedicated following by combining their corporate logo with delicious food. I once sold a company on the idea of giving a sample bread board gift, by saying, "Not only are the breads delicious, but that cutting board will sit for years on their kitchen counter with *your* logo." Promotional product companies have a wide variety of merchandise that can be packaged together with your foods. See the Resources section on the CD for listings of promotional product companies.

For the Holiday Season

Specialty Christmas Breads

Stollen   Scandinavian Braid   St. Lucia's Wreath

Cakes Decorated for the Holidays

Sugar Plum Cake   Carrot   Double Chocolate   Coconut
Red Velvet   Kirschtorte   Chocolate Raspberry Truffle Torte

Cheesecake with our own cookie crust

Chocolate   Real New York Cheesecake   Rum Raisin

Sweetbreads

Banana   Pumpkin   Cranberry   Sour Cream

Southern Fruit Tart

Peach   Strawberry   Raspberry

Tennessee Whiskey Fruitcake

For people who don't like fruitcake, these are made with fresh and
dried fruits only. Order early. We sold out last year!

Cookie Trays   No factory made cookies here

If you haven't seen our trays, you're in for a real treat!

Gift Bags and Baskets

A wonderful way to say
"Thank You"   "Happy Holidays"   "Thinking of you"

Call early to reserve your order: 555-555-5555

SELF-COUNSEL PRESS — START & RUN A HOME-BASED FOOD BUSINESS 09

HOLIDAY LETTER

May 15, 20--

Ms. Charlene Owner
47 Corporate Lane
Businesstown, Anywhere 12345

Dear Ms. Owner,

It's never too early to think about holiday gift giving for your corporate clients. Christmas is coming and you will need to find the perfect business gift. What better way to say thank you and share the joys of the season than by giving your clients a gift basket, gift bag, or cookie tray? We will be happy to help you select a tasty treat your clients won't forget. These delicious delights are all made in our licensed kitchen.

A locally produced homemade gift is more personalized than a commercially produced item and our delicious gifts express a warm, thoughtful feeling in a season of holiday and family cheer.

Create unique items for your clients or choose from a tried and true variety. New this year — we're working with a supplier to offer you custom logo breadboards wrapped with a loaf of our seasonal breads. Your customers and clients can enjoy a true homemade gift of the season and then have a handy cutting board, with your company logo, to use throughout the year.

Thank you for your time and consideration. I will call you next week to set up a short meeting, and I promise to bring samples of my divine delights.

Sincerely,

Marge Deener
Deener's Divine Delights

Chocolate Cake

Preheat oven to 350°F and grease a 9 x 13 pan (or line with parchment).

Mix the sugar, flour, cocoa, baking powder, baking soda, and salt; set aside.

In a separate bowl, beat together the eggs, milk, oil, and vanilla extract. Add the dry ingredients and beat until no lumps are visible. You can use a mixer or beat by hand.

Pour in the last cup of liquid and gently mix until thoroughly combined. This will be thinner than most cake batters. Pour into prepared pan and bake for approximately 30 to 40 minutes.

The cake is done when gentle pressure on top leaves no imprint, the sides of the cake pull away from the pan, and a toothpick (I prefer a sharp knife) inserted into the center comes out clean.

Cool before storing. Keeps for up to one week at room temperature, two weeks in the fridge, or six months in the freezer.

For variations of this recipe see the file on the CD:

Cakes

2 cups sugar

1³/₄ cups flour

³/₄ cup cocoa

1¹/₂ teaspoons baking powder

1¹/₂ teaspoons baking soda

1 teaspoon salt

2 eggs

1 cup milk (or buttermilk)

¹/₂ cup oil

2 teaspoons vanilla extract

1 cup strong coffee
(use water, if that's easier; or even part liquor)

Chapter 10
Promoting Your Products

There are traditional ways of promoting products to start or increase sales. Businesses commonly use a mix of advertising, promotion, marketing, publicity, and public relations. These terms have similar meanings (and are often used interchangeably), but they are not the same. Understanding the differences can help you target the best method of bringing in business for your type of products.

Remember that any action you make is bound to draw in a lot of business, something you might not appreciate when starting up and working from your home. If your business is not yet legal, any form of exposure will only increase the chances that you will get caught. If you have a business license and a health permit, however, these are ways to help bring a product to the attention of potential customers or increase your business with current customers.

1. Create a Logo

You don't need to have a logo for your business, but it gives the consumer an immediate picture of what your business does. A logo, along with a name, makes your business look legitimate, professional, and uniquely "you."

No artist is necessary to create a logo. A distinctive font or royalty-free clip art can work. You could try using a basic line drawing; for example, a baker's cap, a fork and knife, or a steaming platter next to (or incorporating) your business name.

My simple logo was a baker's cap leaning against the left side of my first name; my next shop used my name and the cap, but inside a rolling pin. Now that I only do consulting and teaching, I use my baker's cap logo with my full name.

Use your logo repeatedly on labels, packaging, flyers, and signage. This is called *branding* your product. If you're thinking about selling more than a few muffins from your small business, it helps customers become familiar with your products.

2. Advertising

When we hear the word "advertising," we usually think of media ads that tell us about a product. This has been the most traditional form of advertising, but ads are expensive. Alternatively, you can create brochures, flyers, and direct mailings; email messages such as newsletters or announcements; or use personal contact (word of mouth) to advertise products.

If you decide to pay for advertising, make sure your market is clear and those potential customers are targeted by the ad. Putting your name on plastic covers for a phone book or on the paper placemats in a diner can reap more benefit for the ad salesperson. Ask yourself the following questions:

- Who am I targeting?
- What does my target market read, listen to, or watch?
- Where do my potential customers congregate? In other words, am I selling the type of product that needs to be advertised to this particular market?

Use your common sense and don't let an advertising salesperson pressure you into spending money that can be better used elsewhere. Remember, you have a small, home-based business. Cookies and muffins are more of an impulse item and will probably be purchased not because someone saw your ad, but because he or she happened to be hungry and standing there when your product was close by.

3. Marketing

Traditional marketing uses a wide variety of activities that include advertising, promotion, product pricing, market research, competitor analysis, customer service, and customer satisfaction.

All of these together help a business to target their market for greater sales. You don't need to embark on a formal marketing strategy. The best and simplest marketing plan can be to read the tips included in this book.

4. Publicity

Publicity is free advertising which occurs when your products and/or business are mentioned in the media or within an organization. If you donate to a special activity promoted by a local community group, you should receive free publicity — your business name should be listed in their pre-event advertising, and again during the event.

Product demonstrations or hands-on workshops are another way to introduce your business to the public. Craft fairs, street markets, and farmers' markets — places where you can sell your goods — often have demonstrations. If these venues don't have demonstrations, make the suggestion that they start having them and offer to do one. Adult education programs, community colleges, and service organizations are also good places to do workshops. Call and offer your services!

Don't forget to bring business cards and brochures to events; chat with the assembled groups and let them know who you are. If or when they ever do need your service (or they know someone who does) they are more likely to call a business they know — and since you have introduced yourself, they already know you!

4.1 Press releases

You can also try writing press releases. Why should the newspaper print your story? For the best results, think like a reporter. Write something that will make the reporter's job easier. What's new, interesting, or different? How does your business benefit the community?

A press release is a great way to receive free advertising if you have something unique to say. Perhaps you're having a demonstration or tasting event where you're part of a program and want advance publicity, or need to inform people about a charity or nonprofit event (or some way that you are donating time or products and helping the public).

There's a standard format for press releases. The words "for immediate release" (or whenever it is to be released), must appear in the top right-hand corner. Begin the press release with a hook, or something to catch the readers' attention. Make it brief, with only basic information, and add your contact information. See Sample 17. The CD includes a press release template for your use.

5. Public Relations

Public relations includes ongoing activities to present your business and products in a favorable way. Every time you communicate with the public in any form, you are involved with public relations. A smile and positive words can be your cheapest and most effective strategy. Your family members, friends, neighbors, coworkers, employees, and customers can all help your public relations campaign.

Doing your own public relations can be relatively inexpensive, simple, and an easy way to promote your products. The following sections describe ways for you to do your own public relations campaign.

5.1 Brochures

Brochures are promotional materials that tell people about your business. They can be made of a simple sheet — often folded in thirds, but sometimes in half or quarters — that touts your philosophy, unusual ingredients, or anything that makes you special or different.

List your best qualities and if your local authorities allow it, use key words or phrases such as handmade, home baked, home style,

natural, fresh, unrefined, vegan, sugar-free, or chemical-free.

Flaunt your product and be proud! You don't have to include prices or dates; if you exclude them, so you can continue using the same brochures for a long time.

Your brochures can be printed by a professional service, but most home computers have software capable of making nice ones. If you make your own, remember to proofread carefully. Simple clip art is also a nice addition. Basic white paper is okay, but a soft background color helps to make a brochure stand out. If you opt for adding several print colors, check out the copy prices at your local office supply stores. It might be less expensive to have the clerk print your copies as opposed to using up your own printer cartridge ink.

5.2 Flyers

Flyers are usually one sheet handouts used for short-term information. They include menus, price lists, and order forms which are especially helpful for holiday and special occasion items. Flyers look best with a lot of white space so they are easy to read. You saw a few flyer examples in Chapter 9, and Sample 18 is another variation to give you an idea of what to create.

5.3 Business cards

Business cards are not a necessity, but they are a nice touch that adds a professional look to your business. They are easy to carry and distribute, and can be made at home on your computer.

Keep your business card simple and uncluttered with lots of white space. People only want to know the basics. Use a flyer or brochure for more detailed information. The font should be simple and easy to read with your business name and logo in a larger font.

FRANKIE'S FRESH FOODS

Contact info:
555-555-5555
555-555-4444
frank@frankies.com

FOR IMMEDIATE RELEASE

SUPPORT YOUR LOCAL BUSINESSES

When the mill closed and many of our fine townsfolk lost their jobs, Frank Mitchell turned to his culinary skills to create a new job for himself and two employees. Frankie's Fresh Foods is a new, fully licensed, and local supplier. Mitchell has lived in our community for 25 years. Let's welcome Mitchell's new business and support his entrepreneurial skills.

Marcy's Market, the Big D Superette, and Jason's Corner Store now carry Frankie's Fresh Foods, real homemade dinner items in convenient grab and go containers. No more wondering what you'll make for dinner after a long day at work. No more purchasing fast food with little nutritional value. Enjoy a delicious homemade meal while knowing your dollars will stay right here in our community.

For more information or to schedule an interview, contact Frank Mitchell at 555-555-5555.

Margie's

~~~~~~

Baked Daily

For a taste of Saturday morning heaven,

visit us at the downtown market

SCONES & MUFFINS $1.50
Blueberry Bumble • Crazy Currant • Chocolate Chippies
Wacky Walnut • Pumpkin Parfait • Raisin Baisins

MUFFIN LOAF $5.75
COFFEE CAKE 6"/$8

DROP COOKIES $10.00/lb
Chocolate Chip • Peanut Butter • Gingersnap
Oatmeal Raisin • Snickerdoodle • Chocolate Midnight

Mini Cupcakes $1.25 each or $12.50 dozen
Large Cupcakes $2.50 each or $25.00 dozen

Our products sold at all SuperDeli locations,
the Saturday downtown Farmers' Market, and by calling us:

~~~~~~

Marge and Ernie 555-555-5555

Free Delivery within city limits

Information to include on your business cards:

- Business name
- Logo, if you have one
- Slogan, if you have one
- Add your name and position (e.g., Brownie Smith, owner)
- Contact information, including a phone number, fax number, email address, and website. For a home business, do not add a street address unless you want strangers showing up at your home at all hours of the day. If the business is outside the home where customers can pick up your products, then include a business address.

5.4 Websites

A website is a terrific way to create a strong bond with customers by letting them get to know you and your business. It allows you to keep customers updated on new products, and can allow them an easy way to be in touch with your business.

If you decide to have a website, don't underestimate the importance of having a professional appearance. This does not mean you must hire a professional web designer! It means your site must be updated to reflect an ongoing business (e.g., no Easter bunny cookies advertised in September) and the information must be free of mistakes.

You can learn website design by taking a class, reading a book, or purchasing software. Some businesses even use simple blog publishing to promote their businesses.

5.5 Portfolio

A portfolio is a portable book of pictures of your best-looking products. If you make specialty cakes or any one-of-a-kind products, take pictures and put them in a photo scrapbook. Don't crowd the pictures by putting too many pictures on one page. Also, make sure the pictures are labeled.

When you have a retail table at markets and fairs, prominently display your book. The portfolio is also useful when calling on potential wholesale customers.

5.6 Coupons

The public loves a good deal! Five cents off their next purchase and hip-hip hooray! If you decide to use coupons, make sure to be clear about the terms, including price, product, and expiration dates.

If you have a regular table at the farmers' market or a delivery lunch service, make your own coupons (e.g., good for a small drink with the purchase of a sandwich), and hand it to your customers or slip it into their bags.

5.7 Write your own ads

Target a specific market and think about ways of reaching it by writing your own advertisements, which is a relatively low-cost (sometimes no-cost) form of advertising. Weekly community newspapers, employee newsletters, church bulletins, or bulletins for social and service groups such as Junior League, Kiwanis, Rotary, or Lions Clubs all have a local readership.

5.8 Point-of-purchase promotional materials

Point-of-purchase promotional materials (e.g., tent fold-up cards, flyers, full-color posters, anything that's eye catching) can be placed near your products to attract customers. This works well on your own table display at fairs and markets, but also works in small stores that carry your goods.

You could also use shelf talkers, which are small cards or signs placed under the product and stick out from the shelf to attract attention.

5.9 Promotional products

If you have the money, purchase inexpensive promotional items with your business name on them for giveaways. The intent is to have your name in front of people when you are not there. Examples are plastic cake cutters, refrigerator magnets, can and bottle openers, kitchen towels — anything that people might keep and regularly use or see. For holiday sales, a loaf of bread on a cutting board with your logo will be a yearly reminder that you make delicious homemade breads.

Product labels can be part of your ongoing promotion. If you have enough sales, consider using pressure-sensitive labels or a large custom logo stamp on bags and boxes.

5.10 Newsletters

Many businesses send electronic newsletters, which are simple (just like writing a letter, but watch out for typos) and free. It's a great business tool for keeping in touch with customers. You can announce new products, send coupons, let them know about upcoming events and holidays, and generally remind them that your business is always available to serve their needs. Keep a list of your customers, with their email addresses, and send them periodic updates.

Note that you must give customers the option to unsubscribe from promotional emails. You should follow the regulations set by the Controlling the Assault of Non-Solicited Pornography And Marketing (CAN-SPAM) Act in the US and the *Personal Information Protection and Electronic Documents Act* (PIPEDA) in Canada.

Red Velvet Cake

Preheat oven to 350°F and grease a 9 x 13 pan.

Cream the butter and sugar, then beat in the eggs and vanilla extract.

Stir together the dry ingredients and set aside. In another bowl, combine the liqueur and buttermilk. Alternate adding the liquid and dry ingredients to the butter mixture. The batter might appear curdled; it should be fairly dense and plop from your utensil. If it's too loose, add extra flour.

Spread into the prepared pan and bake for approximately 35 to 45 minutes, until the top is brown and feels solid when lightly pressed. The sides should pull away from the pan, and a knife or toothpick inserted in the center of the cake should come out dry and clean.

Chill before icing. This cake is typically iced with a cream cheese frosting, but buttercream or white chocolate icing is also delicious.

Keeps for up to five days at room temperature, ten days in the fridge, or six months in the freezer.

For variations of this recipe see the file on the CD:

Cakes

1 cup (2 sticks) butter

1½ cups granulated sugar

2 large eggs

1 tablespoon vanilla extract

½ cup buttermilk

1 cup red-colored nut liqueur (if you can't find red, add 1 tablespoon red food coloring)

2½ cups all-purpose flour

3 tablespoons cocoa

2 teaspoons baking powder

½ teaspoon baking soda

½ teaspoon salt

Chapter 11
Using and Measuring Ingredients

Your baked goods will only be as good as the ingredients they contain. Make choices based on the customers you are seeking, but it is always important to use only fresh ingredients. For example, I always taste nuts to make sure they're not rancid; when I use whole grain flour, I make sure it's fresh. When it comes to freshness, never compromise by using old or stale ingredients.

You don't always have to use the most expensive ingredients available. Your choice depends on your customers and whether you think it impacts their decision to buy your products.

I once exchanged cookie recipes with a local bakery. I received their basic sugar cookie recipe and they got my peanut butter cookie recipe. Later, they asked in a rather suspicious tone why my sugar and peanut butter cookies tasted far better than theirs. After questioning them I learned that they had used margarine instead of butter, imitation flavor instead of pure vanilla extract, and a subgrade peanut butter. After we discussed the ingredients they understood why the cookies tasted so different, even though we had used the same recipes. Their

bakery, however, was in a high-traffic shopping mall at which they sold far more cookies than I did and so they had no motivation to change.

When people try my baked goods, they often seem amazed at how great everything tastes. Some people ask, "What's the secret?" I don't consider using good quality ingredients (e.g., real butter, real chocolate, and real vanilla) to be a "secret." Using real fresh or dried fruits instead of the less-expensive imitation fruit bits (sometimes called fruit-flavored additions or gum bits) also makes a difference.

1. Availability and Substitutions

If you're basing a business on a single product, it would be smart to have a substitution contingency plan for any important recipe ingredient. For instance, if you're selling Macadamia Nut Granola, can you easily switch to another nut if it becomes unavailable or the price rises dramatically? Or if you make the most fabulous Cranberry Oatmeal Cookies, but one year the cranberry crop is sparse, are you more willing to pay triple the price or substitute another fruit?

Sometimes switching brands can make a negative difference in your final product. Even when you stick with the same brand, food manufacturers can change a product formula without notifying customers. Margarine is an excellent example: The water content or the percentage of oil can be increased to keep the product profitable for the company but the difference in moisture level can change your final product. Flour can also change: The moisture content and protein levels may differ even though the package has not changed.

The best defense is to become familiar with every recipe and watch for changes in your batter and dough. If you suspect anything, bake a small amount before baking a large amount for sale. If there's a problem, you can make adjustments.

2. Use Natural Ingredients to Extend Shelf Life

The longer your baked goods taste fresh, the longer they can sit on the shelf and make money. Large manufacturers use chemicals to prolong shelf life, but there are natural preservatives available to the home baker. Honey and corn syrup retain moisture. Vinegar is a natural mold inhibitor. Raisins are both a humectant (i.e., help to retain moisture) and a mold inhibitor. Products with high amounts of sugar tend to retard mold and bacteria, and the sugar acts as a dough tenderizer. Chapter 12 will show how these ingredients can be used effectively.

3. Use Fresh Ingredients

Most ingredients will be fine to use for your products but use your common sense if there seems to be any question about freshness.

Whole grain flours, nuts, and seeds can be the worst offenders, sneaking by when you think they're still good. Before using, smell the flours and taste the nuts and seeds. Buy these from a store with a high turnover of products. After several bad experiences, I will now only purchase these items from the bulk bin at my busy local natural foods store. It's a bit more expensive but I haven't had any problems with freshness.

Unless you use the ingredients quickly, store them in the fridge or freezer. A rancid ingredient will ruin your baked goods and reputation.

4. Find a Multifunctional Recipe

You need a good recipe once you have decided on a product and have reviewed contributing considerations (i.e., ease of production, general cost, shelf life, labels and packaging, storage, and transporting).

Begin with a recipe that's simple and problem-free. If it passes your initial bake test, think about how you can refine or make changes. Ask yourself the following questions:

- Does my creation need to look more appealing?

- Do I need to reduce the final cost?

- Is packaging a problem?

Look at each issue the questions bring up and try being creative with your solutions. At this point, feedback from others can be helpful. Opinions are valuable and can sometimes lead to new and interesting ideas.

When I look at recipes, I think about multifunction. A plain recipe that can be used for several products is the most appealing. If my basic yellow cake can be adapted for carrot cake, it means I'm familiar with how it bakes,

I know what to look for during production, all the basic ingredients are in my kitchen, and my scheduling is more flexible. If a customer orders a small carrot cake, I don't have to spend time making a specific batter but can simply take some of my yellow cake batter and stir in carrots, spices, and any other additions.

Having a multifunctional recipe also depends, of course, on your batter capacity and sales amount of any particular product. My first poppy seed cakes were made by adding some seeds to a yellow cake batter. When my sales increased for both poppy seed and yellow cakes, I developed a different, oil-based poppy seed cake, which has its own excellent qualities. It's very fast to mix and has a lovely split on the top which makes an attractive appearance. Now I have an oil-based and a butter-based yellow cake recipe, and both are flexible enough to be used for several products.

5. Increasing the Ingredients

Before you scale up (increase) a recipe size, make sure you bake it at least once. If it's already part of your repertoire, go ahead and double the ingredients.

If it's an unfamiliar recipe, I suggest you do a trial run. Note that cookbook and Internet recipes are notorious for not being thoroughly tested. Everyone bakes differently, be it the way they measure ingredients, select the brands of their ingredients, or by their choice of oven. A new recipe might need adjustments to work properly for you. Baking the recipe will familiarize you with how the batter or dough looks, tastes, and reacts.

If your test batch is successful, start to increase your recipe size. If you decide to make changes, begin with a small batch size because a change might not work the way you expect. Once you have success, double your recipe and bake it. If you find your mixer can handle a larger batter or dough, increase it again, either by doubling it or by adding the original size to the doubled batch.

I have years of experience with recipe and product development and I've learned that shortcutting this step can be costly in time and money. I quadrupled an especially expensive chocolate hazelnut cake recipe for a wedding rehearsal without first familiarizing myself with its properties. I hadn't realized the specialty chocolate would impact the bake temperature and time. The bottom of the cake was so scorched it was inedible. After that, I made this rule: double, then double again. This rule has since saved me money and aggravation especially for new recipes.

When you scale up a recipe, your equipment and preparation time will change based on the volume of the food. Larger batches will need bigger mixing bowls, larger or extra baking pans, will take longer to prepare, and will need more time to bake, cook, and chill. For example, a small candy recipe might need only 10 minutes to "stir constantly," but multiply the original ingredients 16 times and expect to be stirring for quite a while. An 8-inch birthday cake might bake for 30 minutes, but when it becomes a 14-inch wedding cake tier, the cake may need to bake for two hours at a reduced temperature.

A larger recipe also means that you will spend more time packaging, labeling, and putting everything away.

6. Formatting Recipes

You might make the same amount each time you do a recipe, but there will be times when the amount of each product will change. (Doubling a recipe in your head is sure to bring trouble.)

You can write each batch-size recipe on a separate sheet of paper or index card and work from the correct recipe; or create a grid recipe with all the ingredients' names in a column on the left, with separate columns for different yields. See Sample 19.

Laminate your recipes to keep them clean (you won't, however, be able to make notes or changes over lamination), slide each one into a plastic sheet protector, or slip the recipe or cookbook into a large, clear plastic bag while you are using it.

Always keep your recipe near your work area, checking the amounts needed for each product as you move along. It's very easy to get distracted and forget an ingredient. I've used two different techniques that help:

1. Line up all your ingredients and move each ingredient to the side as you use it.

2. Say the ingredient out loud as you add it to the batter. Hearing it will help you remember.

Once you begin a professional business, it's important that all products come out the same each time. Customers will be slightly forgiving since your items are homemade, but they still expect that a cake or bread is going to taste the same each time and that the size will be comparable to the previous purchase. Your serving sizes must be consistent, especially if you are selling individual items.

Portion control ensures customers always get the same amount and that you make the same amount of profit with each serving. For portion control of items such as cookies and muffins, commercial ice cream scoops are excellent tools. You'll have to decide the best size for your products, but by using a scoop you have an easy way to get a consistent measurement.

For cakes and pies, a scale is invaluable for weighing batter and dough.

7. Tweaking a Recipe

Many recipes can benefit from a reduction in sweetener. If a product is too sweet, it overshadows subtler, underlying flavors and diminishes the potential of your wonderful baked goods. In a small batch, try reducing the sweetener by 25 percent and ask family and friends for feedback.

If you would like to increase shelf-life and prevent your goods from drying out too quickly, add one or two tablespoons of a humectant such as honey, corn syrup, or molasses (if the flavors will work). Make sure to reduce the sugar accordingly.

For making healthier products, substitute a small amount of whole wheat pastry flour for the white flour, but only in small quantities. After test baking, add or subtract as needed.

If your ingredient label (and nutrition label, if using one) is important to your customers' health interests, it's possible to tweak a recipe to reflect their concerns. For example, if customers prefer less sweet cookies and don't want to see sugar as the first ingredient, whittle down the amount of sweetener used (e.g., it was originally 2 cups sugar and you've reduced it to 1½ cups), then divide the remaining amount of sugar between granulated sugar and brown sugar, or honey, or use whatever appeals to you. Since each ingredient needs to be listed separately on the label, the amount of each sweetener is now only ¾ cup, and moves further down the label list.

8. Testing Product Shelf Life

It's important to know how long each product will stay fresh and of high enough quality to sell. When testing a recipe, take a few samples, wrap well, label and date the product, and store for a period of time. Most cakes should be tasted every day for quality, but some products like

RECIPE FORMAT

Almond Chocolate Chip Cookies

Ingredient	Yield 1½ dozen	Yield 3 dozen	Yield 6 dozen
butter, softened	½ cup (1 stick)	1 cup (2 sticks)	2 cups
shortening	½ cup	1 cup	2 cups
almond paste	½ cup	1 cup	2 cups
sugar	1 cup	2 cups	4 cups
eggs	1	2	4
almond extract	1½ teaspoons	1 tablespoon	2 tablespoons
flour	2 cups	4 cups	8 cups
baking powder	¾ teaspoon	1½ teaspoons	1 tablespoon
salt	½ teaspoon	1 teaspoon	2 teaspoons
chocolate chips	1 cup	2 cups	4 cups
chopped almonds	½ cup	1 cup	2 cups

biscotti can be left untested for two weeks. With each recipe you must judge what time frame or interval is needed. If the initial taste is good, wrap the rest (it's tempting, but you don't have to eat the entire piece), make a dated note about quality, and put it away again.

When you settle on that product's shelf life, write a note on the recipe. Initially you might remember the details, but I've learned that when you have numerous similar items, a written note is better than a business owner's overfilled memory.

8.1 Freezing your products or ingredients

Freezing fully baked products can be of tremendous help, but most batters and doughs can also be frozen. Make sure to leave room for expansion, wrap well, and label with dates and product names.

Cake and muffin batters should be used within a couple of weeks, thawed in the refrigerator and thoroughly stirred before portioning. Some chemical leaveners lose a slight amount of action over time but not enough to make a significant difference. Unbaked yeast products don't freeze well; baked yeast products do.

9. Measuring Ingredients

As scratch bakers, we all bake differently. The single biggest difference in how we each follow a recipe is in how we measure ingredients. Even for those who believe in precise measurement, a minor difference can sometimes produce a different appearance, taste, or texture. Whatever your style may be it's important to learn each recipe and be consistent in how you measure.

Flour is the most difficult ingredient to measure consistently, for two major reasons:

1. The light powdery volume can vary from one cup to the next cup.

2. As consumers, we are not aware of contributing factors that have to do with growing, reaping, and storing methods, in addition to changes in flour's moisture content.

Again, your best defense is to learn the appearance and texture of your batter and dough so you can always compensate by making adjustments based on knowledge.

If you haven't put much thought into weighing your dry ingredients, please give it careful consideration. It might seem too odd, or just unnecessary for your baking style, but there are benefits to using a scale when you're working professionally. After using a scale regularly, I would never return to baking without one.

10. Utilizing the Leftovers and Excess Products

For a small business with limited income, there are very few things as annoying as having extra baked goods around that you can't sell. The initial joy of surplus cookies can eventually make even the kids get tired of "the same old thing."

Having leftover stales and excess products is an accepted problem with bakeries. The baking industry has developed recipes to cope with the problem. Unsold goods are often toasted, made into crumbs, and then incorporated into other recipes. This is the basis for a popular Spanish Spice Bar Cake originally developed by the A&P supermarket chain. The basic method is to mix a recipe, add dried cake, cookie, and/or sweet dough crumbs, and incorporate enough moisture to compensate for the additional ingredients. If you try this, remember that every recipe is different, so you'll need to experiment. I frequently used this method

with muffins. For example, if I had one dozen extra raisin bran muffins, I crumbled and added them to the next batter along with extra water. I guessed on the amount of water because I was familiar with the batter. I also added an extra pinch of baking soda.

Dried cake crumbs can also be used for decorating cakes instead of using nuts or sprinkles. Take pieces of cake, scrape off any buttercream or filling, and toast the cake pieces in the oven on low until they feel dry and crumbly. Use a food processor, blender, rolling pin, or hammer to make fine crumbs. Use these as you would any nuts or sprinkles.

Can you think of recipes that use store-bought cookie crumbs? How about recipes using graham cracker, vanilla, or chocolate wafers? What about rum balls or cheesecake crusts? Substitute your own ground cookies and adjust flavors. Use crumbs for the bar treat known by various names such as seven layer bars, magic layer bars, Congo bars, or Hello Dolly bars. Your own cookies will make these treats even tastier.

Be careful, however, of mixing highly spiced cookies in with other flavors that might not be compatible. Do testing before using crumbs. I was initially wary about mixing peanut butter with sugar or chocolate chip cookies, but there was never a flavor issue. I did keep gingersnap crumbs separate; I kept those in a different bag and reserved their use for similarly spiced products.

If you have freezer or refrigerator space to store crumbs, they can keep for several months. If you keep them at room temperature, they should be okay for at least one month, but taste test before using. If the texture feels dry or stale, that's okay, but you don't want any off flavors.

The one thing to remember when you are using leftovers to complement other food items is to put the information on your ingredient label. Large food manufacturing companies deal with this by adding "may contain the following ... " This might give you a long label, but it is better to include the information and prevent someone with an allergy having a reaction to your product.

11. Ingredient Equivalencies

The following ingredient list is useful for figuring out cost and recipe amounts. Use this as a guide; there might be some differences due to variations in manufacturing, package settling, and individual measuring.

TABLE 1
INGREDIENT EQUIVALENCIES

Ingredient	Amount	Equivalent Volume Measurement
Allspice, ground	1 oz	4½ tbsp
Almond paste	8 oz	Approximately 1 cup
Almonds, chopped	1 lb shelled	3⅓ to 3⅔ cups
Almonds, ground	1 lb shelled	2⅔ to 3 cups
Almonds, slivered	1 lb shelled	4 cups
Almonds, whole	1 lb shelled	4¼ cups
Apple pie filling	21 oz can	2⅓ cups
Apples	1 medium	1 cup sliced, ¾ cup chopped
Apples	1 lb	2 large, 3 medium, 4 small, 2½ to 3 cups chopped
Apples, dried	6 oz pkg.	1 cup dried
Applesauce	16 oz jar	2 cups
Applesauce, homemade	1 lb apples	1½ cups sauce
Apricots, canned	16 oz	2 cups drained, 6 to 8 whole
Apricots, dried	6 oz pkg.	1 cup dried, 1½ to 2 cups cooked
Apricots, fresh	2 medium	½ cup sliced
Apricots, fresh	1 lb	2 cups halves or slices, 8 to 12 medium whole
Arrowroot	1 tbsp	thickens as 2½ tbsp flour
Baking powder	7 oz can	40 tsp
Baking soda	16 oz box	90 tsp
Bananas	1 medium	¾ cup sliced, ⅓ cup mashed
Bananas	1 lb	3 or 4 medium whole, 1⅓ cups mashed
Bananas, dried slices	1 lb	4 to 4½ cups
Berries	1 pint	2 cups
Blackberries	1 lb	3½ cups fresh or frozen
Blackberries	1 pint	2 to 3 cups fresh or frozen
Blackberries, frozen	10 oz pkg.	2 cups

TABLE 1 — CONTINUED

Blueberries	1 lb	2½ to 2¾ cups fresh or frozen
Blueberries	1 pint	2 cups
Blueberries, frozen	10 oz pkg.	1½ cups
Blueberry pie filling	21 oz can	2⅓ cups
Bran flakes	16 oz pkg.	8½ cups
Butter or margarine	1 stick	4 oz, ½ cup, 8 tbsp,
Butter or margarine	1 lb	4 sticks, 2 cups
Butterscotch chips	12 oz pkg.	2 cups
Carrots, fresh	1 lb	5 to 7 med., 2½ cups shredded, 3 cups chopped
Cashews, shelled	1 lb	3¼ cups
Cheese, cottage	1 lb	2 cups
Cheese, cream	3 oz pkg.	6 tbsp
Cheese, cream	8 oz pkg.	½ lb, 1 cup
Cheese, ricotta	8 oz	1 cup
Cherries, canned, tart	1 lb pitted	1½ cups, drained
Cherries, dried, tart	3 oz	½ cup
Cherries, fresh, sweet	1 lb	2½ cups, pitted
Cherries, frozen, tart	1 lb pitted	2 cups
Cherries, maraschino	10 oz jar	25 cherries with stems, 33 without stems
Cherry pie filling	21 oz can	2⅓ cups
Chestnuts, canned	10 oz can	25 whole nuts
Chestnuts, shelled	1 lb	35 to 40 large, 2½ cups, 2 cups pureed
Chocolate	1 oz	1 sq (unsweetened), ¼ cup grated, 1 env. liquid
Chocolate chips	6 oz	1 cup (semisweet or milk chocolate)
Chocolate wafers	20	1 cup fine crumbs
Cinnamon, ground	1 oz	4 tbsp
Cinnamon candy dots	1 lb pkg.	2¼ cups
Cloves, ground	1 oz	4 tbsp
Cocoa, baking	8 oz	2⅔ cups
Coconut, flaked, pkg.	7 oz	2½ cups
Coconut, fresh	1 lb	3 cups grated, 1 medium whole
Coconut milk	15 oz can	1⅞ cups
Coffee, ground	1 lb	80 tbsp, 40 to 60 cups brewed
Coffee, instant	4 oz jar	2½ cups, 120 cups prepared
Corn, creamed, canned	16 oz	2 cups
Corn, kernels, canned	15 oz	1¾ cups, drained
Cornmeal	1 lb	3 cups uncooked
Cornstarch	1 tbsp	thickens equal to 2 tbsp flour
Cornstarch	1 oz	3 tbsp
Corn syrup	16 oz	2 cups
Cranberries, dried	1 lb	3½ cups
Cranberries, fresh	1 lb	4 cups

TABLE 1 — CONTINUED

Cream, whipping	½ pint	1 cup unwhipped, 2 cups whipped
Cream of tartar	1 oz	3 tbsp
Dates, diced, sugared	1 lb	2 ⅔ cups
Dates, pitted	8 oz pkg.	54 dates, 1¼ to 1½ cups chopped
Eggs, whole, uncooked	1 large	3 tbsp
Eggs, uncooked	1 cup	5 large eggs, 6 medium eggs
Egg white	1 large	2 tbsp
Egg white	1 cup	8 large egg whites
Egg yolk	1 large	1½ tbsp
Egg yolk	1 cup	12 large egg yolks
Fennel, seeds, dried	1 oz	4 tbsp
Figs, dried	1 lb	40 medium, 2½ to 3 cups chopped
Figs, fresh	1 lb	12 small, 9 medium, 2½ cups chopped
Filberts, shelled	1 lb	3½ cups
Flour, all-purpose	1 lb	4 cups sifted, 3½ to 3¾ cups unsifted
Flour, cake	1 lb	4⅛ cups unsifted, 4½ cups sifted
Flour, cake	1 cup, sifted	1 cup less 2 tbsp sifted all-purpose flour (⅞ cup)
Flour, pastry	1 lb	4 cups unsifted, 4½ cups sifted
Flour, rice	1 lb	3 cups unsifted, 3½ cups sifted
Flour, rye	1 lb	4½ to 5 cups unsifted
Flour, whole wheat	1 lb	3¾ cups unsifted, 4 cups sifted
Fruit, candied	1 lb	3 cups chopped
Fruit, canned	16 oz	1½ cups drained, 2 cups fruit and juice
Fruit, dried	1 lb	3 cups
Fruit, frozen	10 oz	1½ cups drained
Fruit pectin, liquid	3 oz	thickens 3 to 4 cups of fruit or 2 to 4 cups of juice
Fruit pectin, powdered	1 ¾ oz	thickens 4 to 8 cups of fruit or 3 to 6 cups of juice
Fruit peel, candied	1 lb	2½ to 3 cups chopped
Fruit, pureed	1 lb	2 cups
Fruit salad	1 qt	7 to 8 servings
Gelatin, unflavored	1 envelope	1 tbsp
Ginger, crystallized	1 tbsp.	1 tsp ground
Ginger, fresh, chopped	1 tbsp.	1 tsp ground
Ginger, fresh	1" piece	1 tbsp grated or chopped
Ginger, ground	½ tsp	1 tsp fresh chopped
Ginger, ground	1 oz	4 tbsp
Hazelnuts, shelled	1 lb	3½ cups
Herbs, fresh, chopped	1 tbsp	1 tsp dried, crushed
Honey	1 lb	1⅓ cups
Jam or jelly	18 oz	1⅔ cups
Lard	1 lb	2½ cups
Lemons	1 medium	2 to 3 tbsp juice, 2 tsp grated peel

SELF-COUNSEL PRESS — START & RUN A HOME-BASED FOOD BUSINESS 09

TABLE 1 — CONTINUED

Lemons	1 lb	4 to 5 medium whole, ⅔ to 1 cup juice
Lemon peel, dried	1 tsp	1 to 2 tsp grated fresh peel, ½ tsp lemon extract
Limes	1 medium	1½ to 2 tbsp juice, 1 to 2 tsp grated peel
Limes	1 lb	6 to 8 medium whole, ½ to ¾ cup juice
Macadamia nuts	7 oz jar	1½ cups
Macadamia nuts	1 lb shelled	3⅓ cups
Mace, ground	1 oz	4½ tbsp
Malted milk powder	13 oz jar	2¾ cups
Mangoes	1 medium	1 cup chopped, ¾ cup pulp
Maple syrup	1 pint	2 cups
Margarine	¼ lb	1 stick, ½ cup, 8 tbsp
Margarine	1 lb	4 sticks, 2 cups
Marshmallow creme	7 oz jar	2⅛ cups
Marshmallows	1 cup	80 miniature, 8 regular
Marshmallows, miniature	10½ oz	5½ cups
Marshmallows, large	1	10 miniature
Marshmallows, large	1 lb	65
Marzipan	8 oz	1 cup
Milk	1 qt	4 cups
Milk, evaporated	5 oz can	⅔ cup
Milk, evaporated	12 oz can	1½ cups
Milk, instant dry	⅓ cup	1 cup prepared
Molasses	1 pint	2 cups
Nectarines	1 lb	3 to 4 medium, 2½ cups sliced, 1¾ cups diced
Nutmeg, ground	1 oz	3½ tbsp
Nutmeg, whole	1	2 tsp grated
Oatmeal, quick-cooking	18 oz pkg.	6 cups uncooked
Oats, rolled	1 lb	5 cups uncooked
Oil, vegetable	16 oz	2 cups
Orange juice, frozen	6 oz can	6 cups reconstituted
Orange peel, dried	1 tbsp	2 to 3 tbsp grated fresh peel, from 1 medium orange
Orange peel, dried	2 tsp	1 tsp orange extract
Oranges	1 medium	⅓ to ½ cup juice, 1½ to 2 tbsp grated peel
Oranges	1 lb	3 medium, 1 cup juice
Oranges, mandarin	11 oz can	1¼ cups
Oranges, mandarin	15 oz can	1¾ cups
Peaches, canned	16 oz can	2 to 2½ cups slices drained, 6 to 10 halves
Peaches, dried	1 lb	3 cups
Peaches, fresh	1 lb	4 medium, 2 cups peeled and sliced
Peaches, frozen	10 oz	1 cup slices drained
Peach pie filling	21 oz can	2⅓ cups
Peanut butter	18 oz jar	2 cups

TABLE 1 — CONTINUED

Peanuts, shelled	1 lb	3½ cups
Pears, canned	16 oz can	2 to 2½ cups slices drained, 6 to 10 halves
Pears, dried	1 lb	2¾ cups dried
Pears, fresh	1 lb	4 medium, 2 cups sliced
Pecans, halves	1 lb	4 cups
Pecans, pieces	6 oz pkg.	1½ cups
Pineapple, chunks/crush	8 oz can	¾ cup, ¼ cup juice
Pineapple, chunks/crush	20 oz can	2 cups, ½ cup juice
Pineapple, fresh	1 medium	3 cups chunks or cubes
Pineapple, sliced	8 oz can	4 slices
Pineapple, sliced	20 oz can	10 slices
Pine nuts	5 oz	1 cup
Pistachios, shelled	1 lb	3½ to 4 cups
Pistachios, shelled	1 cup	4½ oz
Plums, canned	16 oz can	10 to 14 plums
Plums, fresh	1 lb	8 to 10 small, 6 medium, 5 large
Poppy seeds	1 oz	3 tbsp
Prunes, dried	12 oz pkg.	54 prunes, 2½ cups
Pumpkin, canned	15 oz	2 cups, makes one 9-inch pie
Raisins, seedless	1 lb	2¾ to 3 cups
Raspberries, fresh	1 pint	1¾ cups
Raspberries, frozen	10 oz pkg.	1 cup with syrup
Rhubarb, fresh	1 lb	4 to 8 stalks, 3 cups chopped, 2 cups cooked
Rhubarb, fresh	2½ lbs	makes (1) 9-inch pie
Rhubarb, frozen	12 oz pkg.	1½ cups chopped or sliced and cooked
Salt	1 oz	1½ tbsp
Sesame seeds	1 oz	3 tbsp
Shortening	1 lb can	2½ cups
Sour cream	8 oz	1 cup
Strawberries, fresh	1 pint	2½ cups whole, 1¾ cups sliced, 24 to 36 berries
Strawberries, frozen	20 oz pkg.	4 cups whole, 2¼ cups puréed
Sugar, brown	1 lb	2¼ cups packed
Sugar, granulated	1 lb	2¼ cups
Sugar, powdered	1 lb	3½ to 3¾ cups unsifted
Sweetened condensed milk	14 oz can	1¼ cups
Sweet potatoes, canned	16 oz	1¾ to 2 cups
Sweet potatoes, fresh	1 lb	2 to 3 whole, 1¾ to 2 cups mashed
Syrup, maple	12 oz	1½ cups
Tangerines	1 lb	4 medium, 2 cups sections
Tapioca, quick	8 oz pkg.	1½ cups
Tofu, firm	1 lb	2½ cups cubed, 2 cups crumbled
Tofu, soft	1 lb	1¾ cups pureed

TABLE 1 — CONTINUED

Vanilla extract	1 oz	2 tbsp
Vanilla wafers	26 wafers	1 cup fine crumbs
Vanilla wafers	12 oz box	88 wafers
Vinegar	12 oz	1½ cups
Walnuts, shelled	1 lb	3½ cups chopped, 4 cups whole
Wheat germ	12 oz jar	3 cups
Whipped topping	8 oz frozen	3½ cups
Yams	1 lb	2 to 3 whole, 1¾ to 2 cups mashed
Yeast, active	¼ oz pkg.	2¼ tsp
Yeast, active	4 oz jar	14 tbsp
Yeast, compressed	.06 oz cake	equal to ¼ oz pkg. dry
Yogurt	8 oz	1 cup

SELF-COUNSEL PRESS — START & RUN A HOME-BASED FOOD BUSINESS 09

Poppy Seed Cake

Preheat oven to 350°F and grease a 10-inch tube pan or 9 x 13 cake pan.

In a large bowl, beat the eggs, oil, sugar, vanilla extract, and buttermilk.

In a separate bowl, combine the flour, poppy seeds, baking powder, baking soda, and salt. Add to the wet ingredients and mix well. This will be a medium-thin batter.

Pour batter into your prepared pan and bake for 40 to 60 minutes, depending on size of pan. The cake is ready when it pulls away from the sides of the pan, has a split along the top, and passes the toothpick test.

Cool at least 10 minutes before removing from tube pan. The 9 x 13 cake can cool completely in the pan.

For variations of this recipe see the file on the CD:

Cakes

3 large eggs

1 cup oil

2 cups sugar

2 teaspoons vanilla extract

1¼ cups buttermilk

3 cups flour

¼ cup poppy seeds

1 teaspoon baking powder

½ teaspoon baking soda

1 teaspoon salt

Chapter 12
Recipe Advice and Tips

Each recipe included in this book and on the CD was chosen for a reason: because it has qualities conducive to easy production, good shelf life, unusual flavor, and/or it's adaptable to numerous variations. Many of these were my best-selling recipes. For your benefit, to easily find an appropriate recipe, I listed them using simple descriptive names.

Each product category in this chapter includes ideas on packaging and variations that are relevant to all the recipes included in that category. The individual recipes on the CD have notes on shelf life, freezing, and further variations specific to that recipe. These notes can be used as ideas for creating or refining your own products. The recipes use volume measurements, because most people bake and cook this way. Once you become comfortable, you can convert your measurements into weights.

Many of the recipes can be included in special diets. Some are already noted as vegan or fruit-sweetened (no sugar added), but there are others that are nondairy, wheat free, egg free, nut free, low-sodium, low-fat, or 100 percent whole grain. Note that the sugar-free recipes use no chemical sugar substitute and are *not* intended for people with diabetes.

For help with learning the baking basics, or technique, or finding more recipes, consult cookbooks and the web. The Internet is also a great place to find new recipes. Check out my website at www.bakingfix.com.

1. Ongoing Problem Recipes or Products

If you have a problem recipe, take action to eliminate the problem. Running a business is hard enough without having irksome issues with recipes. Try evaluating the situation. Is it a taste, texture, or flavor issue? Is it a shelf life or production problem? Does the product get too dry or too soggy in a short period of time? Or is it just an annoyingly inconsistent recipe? Review your steps during production; think about the ingredients and see if there's something you're not doing the same each time. Perhaps it's an ingredient causing the problem.

Whatever the problem might be, spend time thinking about it. Consult cookbooks and ask experienced bakers for help. *Modern Baking* magazine has a question-and-answer section where technical problems are often addressed by skilled professionals. There's no point in living with a problem that has an answer.

1.1 Occasionally good recipes go bad

Everyone makes mistakes with recipes and at some point you probably will, too. After you calm down, decide if the product is salvageable without compromising your standards. Depending on the venue and your customers' expectations, see if you can give it a new name (e.g., a too-moist chocolate cake can become a chocolate pudding cake). If not, use it for recycling into other products, or cut away inedible parts and share the remains with family and friends.

Occasionally, mistakes happen. Consider it the cost of doing business. However, if a mistake happens regularly, do something about it. Consider your personal traits and how they might impact a problem. If you work best at night, do you find these problems happen in the morning? Do these problems happen only when you're racing to meet a deadline? There's no reason to drive yourself crazy. Look for a solution to the problem and move on.

2. General Tips for Recipes

The following tips pertain to all of my recipes included in this book and on the CD, but many of these tips are applicable to recipes in general.

- Do not sift flour, cocoa, or confectioner's sugar unless there are hard lumps.

- Use real extracts and not imitation flavoring for best flavor results.

- Use the right flour for the recipe. A few recipes use cake flour, which is great for creating a delicate texture, but can be expensive. If you don't want to use it, experiment by substituting a reduced amount of all-purpose flour. Unbleached and bleached flour can be interchanged. When whole wheat pastry flour is specified, do not substitute whole wheat bread flour (sometimes called stone ground). The texture, protein, and gluten contents differ and the final products are dramatically different.

- Crush any lumps of baking soda before measuring.

- Pay close attention to your ingredients, especially when you're moving fast or pre-occupied. Mistakes happen. (Especially with baking soda and baking powder. Both are leaveners, white powders, and come in small packages, but with significantly different results.)

- Brown sugar is sometimes simply white granulated sugar with molasses added in. Packaged brown sugar is convenient, but more expensive than making your own. To convert any recipe that uses brown sugar, use one scant cup granulated sugar with one tablespoon of molasses.

- Powdered sugar and confectioner's sugar are basically the same ingredient.

- Buttercream, icing, and frosting are basically the same.

- When cracking eggs, the shell will sometimes jump into the bowl and defy retrieval. To avoid shell shards in your lovely baked goods, don't crack all the eggs into one bowl; first crack an egg into a cup or small bowl and if you see no shell, then add the egg to your batter. Repeat until all your eggs are cracked. This process isolates any stray shell pieces.

- Jams, jellies, and preserves are table spreads. They are adequate for use in your recipes, but they're not formulated for baking. When used as a baking ingredient, they tend to liquefy, bubble, run off the product, and burn easily. If you'll be using a lot of fruit fillings, consider buying commercial-quality fruit fillings, available from wholesale suppliers. These are formulated to withstand high heat.

- The choice between using butter, margarine, oil, or shortening is up to the baker. Each of these ingredients creates a different texture or flavor, so it depends on what you expect from a product. Health issues surrounding these ingredients have changed several times over the years, and costs have fluctuated dramatically, so I just rely on customer feedback and my personal preference. For the most part, if a recipe uses oil, don't make any substitution. Solid fats in any of the recipes included in the book and on the CD can be interchanged without technical baking problems. One thing to keep in mind is that shortening has a different weight-to-volume ratio than butter or margarine, so you'll need to experiment when making a recipe substitution. Also, some brands of margarine have a high water content so they're not good for baking. Look for packages that say "good for baking." Finally, when using butter, I prefer unsalted simply because less salt is always nice. Either one works in all of the recipes.

- For recipes using (liquid) milk, it's possible to replace the milk with water and then add 1/3 cup dry instant milk powder to your dry ingredients for each cup of milk replaced. This method is much cheaper than using fresh milk and saves

space in your fridge. It's also possible to simply use water to replace the milk. Each recipe is different, however, so judge the results for yourself.

- If you don't want to use buttermilk, add one tablespoon of vinegar or lemon juice per cup of milk. (And deduct one tablespoon of milk.)

- None of the recipes I provided call for flouring additions (e.g., blueberries, chocolate chips) before stirring into the batter. Additions sink to the bottom only when they are placed in batter that is not thick (dense) enough to keep them suspended. To correct this problem, add more flour to your next small batch and pay attention to batter density. Then make the appropriate change to your recipe.

- Flouring sticky ingredients is useful for separating them before adding to the batter so you don't have clumps. If your sticky additions clump, use some of the recipe flour.

- Make up dry mixes. These are the dry ingredients from a recipe that you have already measured and placed in a container. Mix as many containers or bags as you will use within a time period; label, date, and store. When it comes time to bake, prepare your wet ingredients and simply dump in the dry.

- Most batters can be completely mixed, placed in containers, and then refrigerated. Before baking, stir the batter and portion as the recipe intructs you. It will be somewhat thicker when cold, which is okay. This method works well if you only need to bake a few items at a time.

- All baked goods lose moisture when baking. If you want to sell a one-pound loaf of bread or cake, determine how much moisture each recipe loses and scale your batter or dough to include this loss. For instance, if your oat and wheat bread loses 2 ounces, scale your dough for 19 ounces, which will cover the 2-ounce moisture loss plus a little extra for margin of error. You definitely need a scale for this method.

- Grease or use pan spray, even for non-stick pans.

- Get into the habit of completely covering all your baked products after they are cool. It won't hurt them to sit out for short periods while you're in production, but cover as soon as you're done. This keeps them fresh, for longer.

- Always think about how you can improve the visual effect.

3. Muffins and Quick Breads

Muffins are an excellent perennial seller. If you find the right outlet, muffins can keep you in business. The biggest drawback is their shelf life, but that's offset by the ease of production since most recipes are fast and easy. To make it even speedier, use dry mixes and refrigerated batters.

Muffins began as low fat and low sugar, but over the years they've morphed into huge, sweet, fat-enhanced cupcakes without icing. Unfortunately, muffins have kept the "good for you" aura despite being nothing more than empty calories. Somewhere around the 1980s, these sweeter and heftier muffins became all the rage and bakeries profited while waistlines expanded.

My recipe for the basic low-fat muffin is what I would call a real muffin. Because of the reduced amount of sugar and fat, they have a limited shelf life, while the cake muffins can last several days. The kinds of muffins you make depend on the business you seek. For people who eat donuts for breakfast, the cake-like muffins will sell fine. But if your business is health or nutrition oriented, look at the low-fat versions. All of the muffin recipes included with this book were my best-sellers.

Note: A medium muffin refers to a 1 1/2" to 1 3/4" base and large refers to the larger "Texas" sized 2" to 2 1/2" base muffin.

Production:

Paper cups will stick to very low-fat muffins. If you use a recipe that has 1 tablespoon or less of oil per each cup of flour, use pan spray on top of paper liners.

A commercial-quality ice cream scoop (these last forever, the less-expensive ones break) works exceptionally well for scooping muffin batter. Scoop size #24 holds less than one-quarter cup, which is a good size for medium muffins.

Packaging:

Sell individual muffins or in packages of four or six for retail sales; use plastic polybags or clear, rigid plastic containers.

Loaves can be baked and sold in ovenable paper bakeware, wrapped individually in clear film, or placed in a clear rigid plastic container.

Variations:

Any of the muffin recipes can be made into either muffins or loaves.

- Bake in individual small bundts.

- Enhancers: Small amounts of cottage cheese and ricotta cheese added to the batter will keep muffins tender for a longer period of time.

- Vary toppings such as sugar, nuts, crumbs, streusel, or anything else that catches the eye.

4. Cookies

I made several items when I baked in my kitchen, but cookies were my "bread and butter." I sold up to 60 dozen large cookies each week. After I mixed the dough using a wooden spoon, a baby-sized bathtub, and aching arms, I spent a lot of time rushing around greasing cookie sheets, scooping dough, panning cookies, heading to the oven with trays of unbaked cookies, pulling out baked cookies, moving hot cookies to wire racks, moving cooled cookies onto the porcelain tabletops, and running to the sink to wash baking trays. I was exhausted by the end of my day. It wasn't until I'd moved into a retail shop that I learned from a bakery sales rep, Irwin, about commercially available paper sheet pan liners. (Thanks, Irwin!)

I learned an invaluable tip from my mom. Everyone loves a deal! Give a price break for a set amount, and not just a baker's dozen when they buy a dozen. For instance, my shop sold cookies for 35 cents each or three cookies for one dollar (this was many years ago). A typical exchange when my mom manned the counter:

Customer: "One cookie please."

My mom: "Only one?"

Customer: "Okay, two."

Mom: "They're three for a dollar."

Customer: "Okay then, three."

Customers' favorite cookie types are chocolate chip, peanut butter, sugar, oatmeal raisin, snickerdoodles, and gingerbread. Take a basic good seller and make yours with a twist. I made several types of chocolate chip cookies such as Amaretto or Kahlúa chocolate chip (both were made with the liqueurs); almond chocolate chip was made with almond paste. My sales increased dramatically after I began using unusual ingredients in a familiar-to-consumer cookie.

The following are some suggestions to consider when preparing and selling cookies:

- Capitalize on current trends and be prepared to change your product when another trend arrives.

- The more visually appealing, the more likely you'll get a sale.

- Note that biscotti and Mandelbrot have an exceptionally long shelf life and have become a coffee shop staple.

- Soft cookies don't stack well; waxed paper between the layers can help. Most soft iced cookies, such as Black and White cookies, don't stack at all.

- Nuts are nice, but add to the expense. Some people are allergic to them; others just don't like nuts. Do what you want, but I opted not to use nuts. That way, there were more potential sales.

- Shortening creates a chewy texture, while butter adds flavor. I often mix the two for the desired result, but it's strictly a personal preference.

Production:

Most dough can be refrigerated or frozen, but let it soften before using. For portioning dough, use an ice cream scoop; the ones with a thumb release work fast and portion every cookie the same size.

Line sheets with foil, silicone mats, or parchment paper to save on washing pans. After each use, wipe down with a clean paper towel and use again.

Keep cookies stored well, preferably airtight, or they will become stale and develop off-flavors. Keep them in large tubs or boxes until they are sent out for sale. If you are fussy, stack them with waxed paper in between so the tops of the cookies don't get full of crumbs, or wrap them individually before storage, if that's how you will sell them.

Packaging:

For retail packaging, wrap half a dozen cookies or more (large or small) in packages or tins. Cellophane bags are decorative and functional for preventing grease from seeping out.

If you're at a market or street fair, keep all cookies in tubs or covered in baskets, and use a waxed tissue paper for handing to a customer. Most people will also want a little bag.

For wholesale accounts, use fold-up bakery boxes for delivery. It may be ecologically ideal to reuse any old thing for transporting, but remember that if the container looks bad, your business will too.

Variations:

- Make small cookies to sell by the pound, by the dozen, or on cookie trays.

- Use string icing, glaze, sprinkles, cinnamon sugar, or colored sugars.

- Dip ends of cookies in chocolate.

- Make sandwich cookies with buttercream or chocolate.

5. Bars and Brownies

Brownies and bars are a nice complement to cookies. Basic chocolate brownies are great sellers; so are blondies. In my experience, fruit bars sell even better, especially since these are easily adaptable to seasonal fruits. If you live near a fruit-producing region, you can take advantage of the eat-local movement.

Production:

If you need to cut the entire pan into pieces without losing that first cut, line the pan with foil, parchment, or a silicone sheet and lightly pan spray. After the brownies have cooled, run a knife around the inside edges to release any batter that might be stuck. Place a cookie sheet (or anything larger than the brownie pan) over the top of the brownies and, holding tightly with one hand, flip over. Set these on your counter and tap the pan if the brownie has not fallen onto the bottom sheet. Sometimes the batter has seeped under the liner and stuck to the pan so you might have to run a knife around the inside edge again.

Once the brownie sheet is released, remove the pan, peel off the liner, place a cutting board or cookie sheet over the brownie bottom, and flip the trio back over. Now you can mark and cut the brownies.

When cutting bars and brownies, use a marking tool or a tape measure for guidance.

Some people trim the edges but I only do this if they're too brown. Keep all trimmings and use in other products as suggested in Chapter 11.

Packaging:

Wrap for individual sale. Brownies tend to dry out quickly so make sure the wrap seals around the entire brownie.

For retail sales, bake in disposable trays and add a small plastic knife before wrapping if you think your customers may need to slice the product.

Variations:

- Sprinkle chopped nuts or jimmies (sprinkles) on top of brownies for added appeal, or use a string icing.

- Fruit bars can be sprinkled with powdered sugar, but test for shelf life since the sugar sometimes disappears into the streusel after a day.

- To dress up dessert or party trays, cut brownies into small squares and cut each square diagonally. Place the triangles at intervals around the other desserts.

- Bake in muffin cups or bake round brownie cakes for special desserts.

- Bake in ovenable paper bakeware or disposable pans and sell as whole desserts or snacks.

6. Coffee, Bundt, and Pound Cakes

Coffee, bundt, and pound cakes are similar to muffins and loaves but are perceived as more upscale and substantial for social gatherings. Customers will typically buy these when they're entertaining rather than for their own consumption. Therefore, it's very important to have a nice presentation since people are looking for something special.

Production:

These cake batters are all very dense. An offset spatula is useful to help spread and level the batters.

Bundt pans, even the nonstick kind, can benefit from a good amount of grease or pan spray.

Packaging:

For retail sale, sell individual pieces in squares or slices, or packages of four to six pieces. Use clear plastic wrap, plastic polybags, or clear, rigid plastic containers.

Bake and sell whole cakes in ovenable paper bakeware, place on cake circles and wrap in clear film, or place in clear, rigid plastic containers.

Variations:

- Many of the recipes in this section can be made into either muffins or loaves.

- Bake in individual small bundts, which are a great impulse item for gift giving since the fancy shape is perceived as a special occasion product.

- Vary toppings such as sugar, nuts, crumbs, streusels, glaze, string icing, confectioner's sugar, or anything else that catches the eye.

7. Other Cakes

You don't need professional pastry chef training to make and sell cakes. However, you do need to understand the basics. If you're interested in this category, you (hopefully) have a feel for the kitchen with some culinary common sense to guide your judgment.

When I began baking, I had no formal training and learned from books. I also signed up for a cake decorating class. On the first night the instructor said, "I just use a cake mix because customers don't care about the cake, it's the decorating they really care about." I looked around the room as 20 eager women nodded in agreement. I was horrified and dropped the class.

After many years I've learned that people have different tastes and standards. Some customers can't afford to purchase products with more expensive ingredients; some simply prefer what they are used to. This is why targeting your market is important.

The recipes in the cake section on the CD are all excellent sellers from both my retail bakery and home bakery businesses. Make ingredient substitutions as suggested to meet the needs of your customers.

Production:

The cake batters included on the CD can all be mixed and refrigerated, but must be used within one week.

Always wash fruit before using. Peeling fruit is a personal choice. I like keeping the peel on because it's healthier and, honestly, it makes production so much easier.

Use parchment paper liners, cut to fit your pans. This allows the cake to cool in the pan and release without sticking.

Without liners, cool for 20 minutes then de-pan and cool thoroughly. If you have trouble getting a cake to release, put it back into the oven for a few minutes to warm the bottom of the pan. This should soften any batter or grease that solidified as it cooled.

Many pastry chefs use simple syrup to moisten cakes before icing. I prefer to use a great recipe with enough moisture and flavor so that the syrup is not necessary. Note that chilled cakes are easier to ice.

Packaging:

For whole cakes, use fold-up bakery boxes or clear rigid containers. For gooey toppings and soft frostings, be extra careful to ensure that your prized cakes arrive looking gorgeous.

If you're decorating and transporting cakes on cake boards, it's best to use a circle at least 1 inch larger than your cake, preferably 2 inches. For example, if you bake 8-inch cakes, use 10-inch circles and 10-inch boxes.

Variations:

- Most of the recipes included are for a 9 x 13-inch pan, which usually equals two 8-inch or 9-inch round cakes.

- A cake does not have to be iced. For a nice presentation, dress it up with a dusting of confectioner's sugar, a sprinkle of nuts, a handful of colorful cake or cookie toppers, or toasted nuts (sliced almonds are pretty).

- The cake recipes also make great cupcakes.

8. Cake Frostings

There are numerous icing choices, but I like to simplify and use the basic vanilla buttercream for almost everything. It's a multipurpose icing that can be easily flavored with extracts, fruits, or chocolate. I make up large batches of the basic vanilla and keep it refrigerated. When I need another flavor, I scoop some vanilla into a bowl and make additions until the flavor is right. Sometimes this necessitates multiple tastings.

Decide which frosting is best for your product from the frosting recipes included on the CD. Remember, it's really a matter of personal opinion. Traditionally, a cream cheese frosting goes on carrot and red velvet cake, but I've never put a cream cheese frosting on either unless a customer requested it. My reason? People tend to leave cakes on their counter for long periods or overnight, even though cream cheese must be refrigerated. When I've said to customers, "You can choose any frosting, but I usually use a real buttercream frosting," they've been satisfied that they were getting the best choice.

9. Pies, Pastries, and Sweet Crusts

People love pie. Too bad pies are fussy to make! Most pastry dough can be intimidating even for accomplished bakers. This section is meant to help you understand the different kinds of pastry dough, their applications, and how they hold up when you're in business (shelf life is important). For pie-filling recipes, consult cookbooks, magazines, and websites.

It might be tempting for you to skip this step and buy the frozen factory pie shells, then concentrate on your fillings. Many restaurants, bakeries, and individuals, even those who advertise "scratch" or homemade products, purchase the shells. You should make the decision based on your market and your personal needs. If you do opt to use a piecrust recipe, crimp around the edge to differentiate yours; but don't build up the crust too high or it will fall off and look unsightly.

Once you learn the pie basics, making them isn't too hard. All the recipes on the CD (except the oil-based pastry dough) can be made in large quantities, divided, and frozen. The oil-based dough gets cranky if you make it ahead of time, but it makes up for itself with its speedy manufacturing time.

Production:

Use lots of flour when rolling the dough. Use a soft pastry brush for excess flour.

Grease your pans, especially if the pie will be cut and sold by the piece.

Packaging:

Whole pies should be made in disposable pans unless a restaurant account will arrange to return your pans.

Individual pies or cut pieces can be wrapped or placed in rigid plastic containers. If you're selling them at a market or street fair, place individual pieces on plates and supply a fork. Have boxes available for whole pies.

Variations:

- Add finely chopped nuts, herbs, or spices to any dough. These additions make it very clear that it's a real made-from-scratch product.

- All the crust recipes on the CD work with savory fillings such as quiche, dinner pies, pockets, strudels, and hors d'oeuvres.

- Pastry and pie dough can be used in a pan of any shape, not just the traditional pie shape.

- Roll out individual pastries for sweet or savory items.

- Use as the bottom crust for bars.

- Double-crust pies are nice, but are more labor intensive and expensive than using a bottom crust with a streusel topping.

10. Breads, Buns, and Breakfast Pastries

If you're a dedicated artisan bread baker, this is a labor of love and you already understand the intricacies of making a labor-intensive, short shelf-life product.

For bread novices, if you read this section and don't understand most of what I wrote, get lots of practice, or simply move on to other categories of baked goods. Baking is hard enough without adding in the special needs of yeast.

The recipes included on the CD are for traditional yeasted loaves in the two-pound size for a bread machine. This small batch size will allow you to decide if it's bread dough you want to work with. If you like the recipe, then start to scale up.

Since bread takes up so much time and oven space, I suggest you fit in other products to compensate for this downside to bread making.

Production:

Vinegar acts as a natural mold inhibitor and preservative. I add one tablespoon per two-pound recipe during warmer weather when baked goods need the extra help.

Dough can be refrigerated for a day or two but will need to be punched down. The warmer the dough, the more often it needs to be deflated, so punch it intermittently, three or four times, until it's cold enough not to need punching down. Each recipe is different, so keep an eye on the dough.

Raw dough doesn't freeze well for more than a couple weeks — cold temperatures kill yeast.

Packaging:

Loaves should be wrapped in polybags with a twist tie.

Package buns together in whatever quantity you choose; people are accustomed to buying several at once. Don't sell buns individually or you'll lose sales.

Variations:

- Bread dough can be used for burger buns, sandwich rolls, dinner rolls, sweet buns, and cinnamon buns.

- There are many varieties of individual pastries such as schneckens, bear claws, and fruit-filled Danishes. Bread dough adapts well to forming these morning treats.

- Make pizza dough or pizza shells.

11. Fruit Sweetened, No-Sugar Added Products

Fruit sweetened no-sugar added products is a niche market. These desserts and snacks contain no sugar substitutes but are sweetened with only fruit products. You have a wide variety of sweeteners to choose from such as juices, jams, fruit butters, and real fresh fruit.

When purchasing ingredients, read the labels carefully since items that are promoted as "Real Fruit!" might also contain added sugars. I've been fooled several times, especially with concentrated fruit juices and dried dates. Some frozen concentrates use high fructose corn syrup, which is just another form of sugar, so these juices should be avoided. Dates are naturally sweet so I use them a lot, but some brands use sugar to coat and separate their chopped variety.

Remember that when you label your products, you must be clear about what your product contains. In addition to advertising "no sugar, fruit sweetened," clarify with "no sugar substitutes" or "no chemical or artificial sweeteners" or "fruit only."

I originally developed the fruit-sweetened recipes on the CD for a company that wanted all-natural diabetic desserts. After I was finished with the product development phase, the company's dietitian worked up the nutritional labeling. Later, I baked several of the recipes in my shop and was quite surprised that they sold better to customers who were on weight-loss diets. Whatever your customers' motivations, these desserts are a nice change from the highly sweetened desserts everyone is used to eating.

Production:

Work quickly, because once the dry and wet ingredients are combined, the batter begins to foam. Have all baking pans ready. If necessary, stir once before panning.

These products will mold rapidly in a warm environment, so keep refrigerated during hot weather.

Packaging:

Package muffins, cookies, or strudel pieces in bags or boxes and sell by quantity rather than individually.

Variations:

- Bake whole cakes in disposable containers.

- All cake recipes included on the CD can be made into muffins or cupcakes.

- Vary the juices; apple and orange juices are usually cheapest, but sometimes their flavors don't blend well with the main desired flavor. White grape concentrate is excellent but comparatively more expensive.

Harvest Cake Muffins

Prepare fruit and set aside.

Preheat oven to 350°F and line the muffin pans with paper cups or use pan spray.

In a large bowl, beat the eggs, oil, sugar, vanilla extract, and buttermilk. In a separate bowl, combine the flour, baking powder, baking soda, and salt. Add to the wet ingredients, mix well until there are no lumps of flour, and stir in the fruit.

Scoop into muffin cups and bake for 25 to 35 minutes, until the tops feel firm when lightly pressed or a toothpick comes out dry.

Cool thoroughly. Keeps for several days at room temperature or for up to six months frozen.

For variations of this recipe see the file on the CD:

Muffins and Quick Breads

Yield: 12 large cake muffins

2-3 cups chopped fresh or dried fruit

3 large eggs

1 cup oil

1^3/4 cups sugar

2 teaspoons vanilla extract

1^1/4 cups buttermilk

3^1/2 cups all-purpose flour

1^1/4 teaspoons baking powder

^{1}/2 teaspoon baking soda

1 teaspoon salt

Chapter 13
Production and Business Tips

I spent years learning by trial and error. I asked lots of questions and picked up new ideas from reading cookbooks and magazines. The following tips have been invaluable to me.

1. Production Tips

In order to make your production go smoothly, you will need to consider a few things. This section will help you organize your production time and techniques.

1.1 Seasonal production

Production issues change depending on the temperature. In the summer, when it's already hot, your oven is pumping even more heat into your living quarters. Rising temperatures affect storage issues (e.g., bugs begin to hatch), batters can ferment if they stand too long, most dough becomes soft, yeasted dough rises too rapidly, and as the temperature rises so does your irritation. Air conditioning is very expensive and not always available. Here are some suggestions to help you cope with the hot season:

- Keep summer hours and bake very early in the day.

- Prepare batter and dough before you turn on the oven; chill until needed.

- Open the oven door as little as possible while baking.

- Chocolate chip cookies need special attention when the indoor temperature rises over 80 degrees Fahrenheit (27 degrees Celsius). Freeze your chips and refrigerate your dough. Be careful when packaging or storing the cookies or the chips will smear.

- Some people develop a seasonal product list to help offset these issues.

- An extra refrigerator or freezer and some room fans would be a huge help, but be wary of fans and flour.

- Dress appropriately; wear light cotton fabric, nothing clingy, and short sleeves or a sleeveless top.

- Always wear covered shoes. You never intend to drop things, but it happens. A hard shoe between your toe and a knife can make a big difference.

Winter production isn't too much of a problem unless you work with yeasted products, which will need longer to rise. Also, if you wear sweatshirts or sweaters while in production, these tend to pick up fuzz and hair, so occasionally take a break and shake them out.

1.2 Scheduling production

Working from home is different from going to a place of work. Not everyone is well suited to working from home. You don't have to get dressed, there's no commute time, and it can feel lonely. More importantly, though, you're the boss and the workload is entirely up to you. If it doesn't get done, it's your responsibility.

Interruptions can eat away at efficiency. Your family members must be aware that you're working, even though you're home. The same goes for neighbors and friends. When customers or suppliers call, be brief and pleasant or just let the answering machine take messages. If you have young children, take their schedules into account. As your business grows, either hire a babysitter, arrange with family or friends to watch the children, or work when children are asleep.

When preparing your production schedule, think about the order of your baking. What makes the most sense? "Multitasking" is the perfect word to describe a time-efficient kitchen manager. Are you making bread with a long rise time? Any orders going out soon? Start those first. If pie dough must chill for 30 minutes, use that time to prep ingredients you'll need for another recipe. While your cakes are in the oven, turn those leftover stale cookies into crust crumbs for next week's cheesecake order. At the end of your baking, turn off the oven and prepare batter and dough, which can be refrigerated until your next scheduled production time.

The conventional home-sized oven can turn out a lot of baked goods, but it does have a limit of how much can be done in a baking session. When you're deciding on products, keep this in mind. The size of bread loaves or the length of time a cheesecake bakes can be a disadvantage. Efficient scheduling and time management can help offset part of the issue. Dovetail different recipes so that if a product will be using the oven space for several hours, schedule a stovetop or no-bake recipe while your items are baking. This would also be a perfect time to do bookkeeping chores. If you are using your home kitchen, you can fit in household chores.

For times when you have a large order, try to vary your work schedule to produce the extra quantity. Perhaps start earlier in the day or bake ahead and store products in the freezer. Utilize shelf life knowledge to bake the longer shelf-stable items ahead of time.

1.3 Assembly line method

Want to save time? Work towards using this efficient approach. For instance, if you're making a dry mix, get all your containers or bags lined up then measure flour for each one, then leavener, spices, etc. When scooping cookies or muffins that need a topping before baking, scoop all your batter or dough before adding the topping.

If you're individually wrapping your baked items one by one, consider how much counter space you can devote to doing as many as possible at one time. Tear off several sheets of your wrap, setting each piece down so that you can easily reach them. Place an item in the middle of each piece, top side down. Then pull the wrap over the bottom, folding as you go until the item is completely sealed. Make sure no air gets to any exposed surface because this shortens the shelf life. Wrap as many as you can at once, then start again until they are all finished.

Tip: To keep in moisture, wrap or cover your baked goods as soon as they are cooled. If left unwrapped, items are susceptible to drying out and to picking up off-flavors, stray dust, dirt, and insects. However, do not wrap anything until it is thoroughly cooled, since excess moisture can encourage mold.

To help you speed production there are a couple of things you can do. Batters can be mixed and refrigerated for up to one week. (Remember to stir before using.) Dry mixes are a big help when you don't have refrigerator space for storing batters. Measure and mix all the dry ingredients for a recipe, and store in plastic bags until ready to use.

1.4 Being organized

If your business only entails making a few cookies or an occasional cake, you might not feel the necessity of keeping a production schedule. But if your business is larger (or grows), organize yourself with a calendar and to-do lists. For a production schedule, use whatever form makes you feel most comfortable; for example, the computer, a paper or dry-erase calendar, or even a large piece of plain paper. On the CD you will find a monthly calendar for your use.

The calendar is different from a to-do list; a calendar enables you to glance at the week and see when and what must be done. It's a great organizational tool and keeps you from forgetting any account or special order. Plan your week. Begin by adding your customer and wholesale orders, then write in everything else that needs to be done.

Take into consideration when you work best (e.g., are you a night owl or early riser?) and always leave a cushion of time to make sure everything gets cooked or baked, cooled, packaged, and delivered. If you like to work at night, go ahead! If you're a morning person, start early. Much depends on when you need to get your products out, especially if they are short shelf-life items. If you use an alternate kitchen, it will be especially important to use your time well.

As your business grows, you will be better able to handle the changes if you're organized. If your schedule begins to fill out, you'll need more than a production calendar. If necessary, use separate daily, weekly, and monthly to-do lists. These methods also help to organize customer orders by separating wholesale and retail customers. Use your computer, purchase a planner, or create your own handwritten lists. I use several 5 x 8 notepads with a different pad for each activity (e.g., one for daily to-do lists, another for long-term projects). If you have a bustling business, it's helpful to create inventory lists for all your goods and separate them by supplier. Use whatever works for you, but use *something* or you'll have trouble when your business grows.

2. Food Safety Tips

I've worked in commercial kitchens and I've been aghast at what some formally trained "professional" pastry chefs would do to foods. Their fruit tarts were gorgeous but they wouldn't spend their award-winning time first washing dirt from fruits; tubs of custard were left un-refrigerated for days because it was more convenient to leave them stacked on the floor; cutting cheesecake involved dipping the knife after each cut into dirty sink water. I sometimes refused to follow their instructions and was ridiculed. (As a way to deflect their "guidance" I began calling myself the "faux pastry chef.") My rule has been, and hopefully yours, too, will be: Don't make or sell anything that you wouldn't eat yourself.

Read and understand all the health department licensing rules for your area and follow them. These rules were not created to annoy you or make life difficult; they were intended to protect the consumer. These are some of the things the rules will tell you to do:

- Always wash your hands before starting your work, and wash frequently in-between.

- Wearing a hairnet or cap or tying hair back can help keep stray hair away from your ingredients.

- Keep thermometers in your refrigerator and freezer, and check them daily. This will alert you to any impending problems.

- Use a meat thermometer if you handle meat or fish products; check guidelines for hot and cold temperatures.

- Avoid cross contamination. If one cutting board is used for meats and poultry, don't use the same one for other foods.

- No animals should be allowed in the production area while you're working. Please, no cats on the counter or dogs sniffing around your open bag of sugar in the dining room.

- Keep insect and rodent issues under control.

- Rotate stock so that the oldest ingredients are used first. Label and check dates.

Important Tip: Only use food-grade packaging for wrapping or storing your products. Garbage bags, which are treated with mold inhibitors and insecticides, should never touch food.

3. Kitchen Safety Tips

You should have a set of kitchen safety rules. It is especially important to create rules for anyone working or volunteering for you. No matter how careful you are, accidents can happen. Accidents can not only hurt you physically but they can also slow down production and cost you money.

Here are some common sense tips:

- Never stick anything into a running machine.

- Never alter a piece of equipment to bypass the safety mechanism.

- Never put a knife, or anything else that's sharp, into a tub or sink of water with other things to be washed. Even if the sink's not filled with soapy water, that sharp object can hide. Set it aside on the counter or someplace plainly visible.

- Pay attention to your surroundings. If you ever think, "that glass jar might fall," or, "this stool might be in the way," take care of those things immediately.

- Don't use water on a cooking fire. Keep a small fire extinguisher in the kitchen. A box of baking soda is an acceptable alternative.

Safety first! Take the time to slow down. Your business depends on it.

4. Business Tips

If your business productivity is fine and you don't have a problem getting work done, then good for you! But for many people, working at home presents unique problems. Mostly, it can allow a person to indulge in counterproductive habits. Watching TV, chatting on the phone, or visiting with friends is okay if you can multitask without these things interfering in production; but they often do take time from work. A task that should have taken an hour can drag on all afternoon.

For the workaholic type, there's the opposite danger of working nonstop. Driving yourself hard is especially easy if you live where you work. Sleeping too late or working too much are opposites but both of these can deplete efficiency.

Your home business is a job and you need to treat it as such. This section includes a few things I've learned along the way, which are valuable business tips to help you stay organized and professional.

4.1 Look professional

Staying in pajamas the entire day can put a person in a sloppy frame of mind. Plus it's bad business having a customer stop by when you're in jammies. Every day, get up, get dressed, and put yourself in "work mode."

4.2 Your food should look professional too

Don't sell anything that you would not eat yourself. Set a standard and hold yourself to it. If something is too brown to be golden, consider how a customer would react to that product. Are you proud of it? Extra confectioner's sugar or icing is not going to mask the flavor of *burned*. This is your reputation at stake.

Realize that some food loss is part of this business. You're building an enterprise based on customer satisfaction. I knew a woman who just gave burned cupcakes some thicker icing. Her business lasted less than six months.

4.3 Organize your home office

Get organized and stay organized. Making a schedule and striving to follow it is part of being organized. Your business consists of countless details that together make up a unique enterprise. If you're not a detail-oriented person, lists will be especially important. Make yourself notes and write lists; it's the only way you'll be able to keep track of all the details.

Set aside work space for your bookkeeping. Even a box next to your computer for holding ledgers and receipt envelopes will make the job easier. At the very least, keep a makeshift file box with all your papers and clear a space to work at the kitchen table. Bookkeeping is an important part of running a business. Without your records, all you have is a hobby.

4.4 Be timely

Return calls, place supplier orders, and fill customer orders on time. If timeliness is a problem in your personal life do not carry this habit over into your business life. It will only hurt your reputation and speed your failure.

4.5 Be consistent

Once you label a product and put it out for sale, your customers expect the same product each time they buy it. If you make a change, you need to add new information to the label of the product; for example, *New and Improved!* You could also turn it into a different product with a new name. Remember, when you take a recipe and make some changes, the commercial industry calls it a *line extension*.

You can do the same thing even if the change started from a mistake. One time my old-fashioned fudge recipe came out too soft because I wasn't paying attention and didn't cook it long enough. We all make mistakes, right? It had to be sold from the refrigerated case. I added string icing and a few chopped nuts, gave it a new name, and a red bow; I sold all the fudge and continued carrying this new product.

4.6 Be a thinker

Always rethink your processes and always look for ways that can improve what you do. How can you be more efficient in your baking schedule? Are there new products that can simplify your life? Look at your business from the customers' viewpoint and see what they see. How can you improve things for them? Always ask questions.

If there's something you don't understand or something you want to do and don't know how, ask. Look at what others are doing, seek answers, and use your common sense. Fit the answer in with what you are reasonably capable of doing. Keep looking for alternative ways of doing business.

4.7 Problem solve

When there's a problem, deal with it immediately. If your oven burns cookie bottoms, resolve the issue by finding an answer to the problem. Do you need a new thermostat, new cookie sheets, or are you opening the oven door too often?

Don't let a problem persist or it will drive you crazy. If your paper bags continually break, find another supplier or a different form of packaging. If a customer is unhappy because they found dog hair in their muffin, apologize, return his or her money, and give the person a fresh muffin for free. Then vacuum and wipe down all surfaces before each bake session and keep your dog out of the production area (that is, your kitchen) while you're working. You do not want a reputation for being dirty.

If a problem is too much to handle, call in an expert. Whether it's bookkeeping, a troublesome product, or a zoning issue, seek help instead of obsessing over the worst possible outcome. Talk with family and friends. Find other business owners that you can discuss issues with, especially if they are in the same line of business. Trade magazines usually have a question-and-answer section where you can ask the professionals for advice.

You could also go to services such as Service Core of Retired Executives (SCORE) or a food-venture business that helps small businesses by providing advice and problem-solving techniques. For specific business-related issues, contact the Internal Revenue Service in the United States, the Canada Revenue Agency in Canada, your bank, or an insurance agent.

Be wary of people, ads, books, or websites that are hawking videos and paraphernalia that claim they're the *only* ones capable of helping people like you. The louder they scream, the faster you need to move on elsewhere. It might be tempting, but it's almost always a scam.

For smaller nagging issues, spend time thinking about them and jot down ideas about how to solve the problems. The important thing is to admit your mistakes, take corrective action, and move on. A mistake is never the end of the world.

4.8 Know your competition

You might regard other home-based food businesses, farmers' market stands, or small local bakeries as your competition. I disagree. The real competition is the factory-produced food product that is sold on supermarket shelves stocked with other commercially prepared foods.

A tremendous amount of support can come from your colleagues. Other home-based bakers face the same issues and problems that you do. Sharing tips and advice, and passing on business that you can't handle, is a very nice way to be in business. Be helpful to each other and be supportive; even putting together a local community group can help all of you survive.

4.9 Donations

Once you're in business, people will solicit donations for cash or product; the perception is that if you own a business, you are rich. Donations can be a great advertisement for your products, but giving away your goods doesn't always reap financial benefits. My rule was to consider requests from customers only.

For cash donations, set limits. However, saying no is fine and you will need to say no many times. You can pick a special charity and donate only to them — maybe it's your religious affiliation, or your child's school, or a nonprofit organization — the choice is yours. This gives you a gentle way to turn people down. You could say, "Yes, I would like to, but I can't donate to everyone." You could also give a little money to several charities you support. If solicitors don't respect your answer, don't let them bully you.

For donations of free products, it's very much the same. Solicitors will promise that this is the best way for you to advertise your business, but it often doesn't work that way, especially if the potential customers don't find your location convenient. I've had a couple of outrageous requests. A local post office asked for a donation for *their* customer appreciation day. A group of women, who met monthly, for a purpose they would not or could not divulge, wanted me to donate for every meeting because "it would be good publicity." Set a standard and hold to it or you will be paying the bills out of your own personal money.

4.10 Don't give away recipes

Don't give away a recipe that is, or might be, part of your product line. This is how you want to make a living. If you gave away your recipes, you would be giving away your income. Besides, if your goods are so great, let people keep buying from you.

Be flattered, but be smart when someone asks you for your recipe. Be firm, smile, and tell the person you're glad he or she likes your products and if you ever stop making them permanently, he or she will be the first on your list for the recipe.

Several times I've had customers request a recipe and then counter my response by adding that they were "moving" or "wouldn't share it with anyone." Don't let those pushy folks steal your livelihood. Remember that your friendly competitors might want your business and your recipes too.

5. Customer Service Tips

Always remember that without customers you would not have a business. Ask them for their opinions. For example, "How can I do a better job? What new products would you like to see or which current products should I improve?" Show them you care and make an effort to earn their loyalty. You will find some great ideas in their suggestions.

5.1 Put on a happy face

It doesn't matter how grumpy you feel or how bad your day is going; if you're in business, you need to keep that grouch from the public. No one likes a sourpuss.

Get used to the question, "How's business?" This is a greeting, not an inquiry into your finances or life problems. You can answer honestly to your closest confidants, but to everyone else say, "Great!" Regardless of how you feel at the moment, business does change, going through ups and downs, but no one likes a loser. Whether you're manning the farmers' market table or making deliveries to your clients, put on a smile or your attitude will ensure lost business.

5.2 Keep in contact

Keep a customer list and send out announcements of new products, new outlets, or a short newsletter. This helps to keep customers interested and loyal. Hopefully, they will spread the word. It's easier to keep an old customer than find a new one.

5.3 Dealing with pushy people

We've all been exposed to the pushy personality type, but get ready for more of this behavior when you have a business. These people only think about themselves and what you can do for them, so be prepared and be firm. They might masquerade as your friend, relative, neighbor, or customer, but don't let them manipulate you into doing what does not feel right.

5.4 Observing your customers

You don't need to employ a mystery shopper, but you can be a mystery shopper yourself when you're selling retail or making deliveries. Always check your display and watch as customers do or don't pick up your products. If possible, ask them questions; this is an important form of market research. Also, ask a few very good friends or reliable relatives to keep you posted on anything they see or hear about your products.

You can also ask for feedback from the manager or employees where your products are sold, since this can benefit their business, too. But remember that they are busy folks with a lot to do.

5.5 Hire good employees

As business increases, see how you can manage by yourself, but don't work so hard that you endure excessive physical discomfort. If you need help, try enlisting family members to pitch in on assigned tasks. The money you earn benefits the entire family. If you still need help, see if there's a neighbor or friend who will lend a hand in exchange for baked goods.

If you have anyone selling your wares, remember that the person becomes your business ambassador. He or she must do things the way you want them done. If the person is working at a farmers' market for you, the display must look clean and neat, and the person must be pleasant to all shoppers. I suggest you find out how the person is doing. Ask a trusted friend or relative to pretend to be a customer, someone unknown to your employee. You have the right to know if your customers are not treated well.

If you hire people to sell your product, deal with the customers, or make deliveries, it's important to hire good-natured, pleasant people. An employee can pretend to be nice to you, but if that's not his or her true nature, the person will almost certainly be rude to your customers and other business contacts.

Occasionally check on employees by asking your outlets if everything is okay. Don't be afraid to ask leading questions such as, "How is my delivery person working out for you? Is he (or she) prompt and courteous? Are there any problems I need to know about?" If you need only occasional paid labor, try using a temporary service. A temporary service company will have bonded and screened employees, and the company will take care of all the paperwork. It might be the simplest method when you need temporary help to keep business going.

If you must hire permanent employees, consider screening and hiring your own workers. When hiring, check references because job seekers will often tell you anything to get hired. Only previous employer references will help you decide who's best for the job. For legal reasons, former employers are afraid to be honest, so be careful about how you phrase your inquiries. Everyone is allowed an opinion, so ask the reference these types of questions:

- "Would you hire this person again?"

- "Knowing what you know now, would you have hired him or her?"

Also look at the candidate's employment history. If it's spotty, then you will be the next entry on the application the person fills out in two months. If the person bad-mouths a former employer, you will be next.

You need to consider the following questions when you are interviewing a potential employee:

- Does this person take responsibility or is everything someone else's fault?

- Does this person have a great reason why he or she didn't give notice when he or she left his or her last position?

Beware of job hunters who are more interested in learning the trade so they can be your new competition. Once an employee is hired, do not share your business details with him or her. Keep the customer list locked away and ditto for your recipes. If you have special recipes, make up a dry mix for each one and use "dry mix" in the recipe instructions so an employee does not know how much ingredients are used.

Tip: Don't let anyone else handle taking orders. If the person gets the order wrong, it's your business problem, not his or hers

6. Taking Care of Yourself

Some of the hazards of running a home business can be caused by increased stress due to lack of organization, not making time for yourself, and isolation. It is important to take care of your business, but it is also important to take care of *you*.

6.1 Prioritize to reduce stress

Once your business is moving along, there's never enough time to do everything, especially if you have a family. A way to reduce stress is to prioritize. As I've said before, keep lists (e.g., daily, weekly, monthly, and long-term lists).

On your daily list, prioritize what needs to be done for the day. Add anything that cannot be put off to another day, whether it's a customer order or a delivery. Do those first or it will cause you immense stress and worry. Anything you can't get to, put on your weekly list.

Make sure you watch for those time wasters. Let the answering machine take messages, send away a chatty neighbor, and don't open your email unless you're expecting something that needs immediate attention. Try this approach a few times and see if it helps you feel less stressed. Sometimes hectic days cannot be helped, but you need to deal with those days in such a way that you don't feel too frazzled.

6.2 Manage your time

Remember to set aside time for yourself. If you're not taking care of you, both you and the business will suffer. It will be important to juggle your time amongst three important entities: your family, your business, and you. Be aware of time wasters and set limits; there's never enough time to do everything, so learn how to say no. After a while I got into the habit of responding to most requests with, "I'd love to, but ... " It keeps a positive spin on things even when you must decline.

6.3 Avoid isolation

For some people, working alone at home can be an adjustment. There is no sense of belonging to a group and no feedback from coworkers or a boss, which can make some people feel lonely. If working alone is hard for you, a partnership may work better than a sole proprietorship.

Find ways to incorporate regular contact with others. Scheduling deliveries two or three times a week might help. There are also organizations catering to work-at-home folks, with message boards where you can post or answer questions. If you decide this can help, just make sure you limit the time you spend talking to others or other problems can arise.

Networking with similar home-based food business owners is ideal. Often, this kind of relationship leads to information sharing such as learning about good suppliers, sales or discounts, ideas for products, and problem solving. Maybe you can even send each other business.

While I was delivering one day I met a competitor, a woman who also sold to one of my outlets. We chatted and liked each other, so we set up regular meetings that helped both of us feel less alone in our ventures.

6.4 Occupational hazards

Be smart about your body. Occasional aches are a natural by-product of manual labor, but too much labor can create long-term permanent troubles. Watch out for back, feet, arm, and hand problems, which are prevalent in the food industry.

Repetitive-stress injury, such as carpal tunnel syndrome, is more often associated with computer work but it can happen to anyone who exerts, or overuses, their arms or hands. I've had several hand surgeries that might have been avoided if I'd paid attention instead of thinking I would "tough it out." Don't wait until you're in serious pain; investigate the problem and look for solutions. For instance, take a ten-minute break every hour when you're decorating cakes, or wear a pair of support hose and take breaks to take care of the issue.

Grand Marnier Fruitcake

Using a nonmetallic stockpot, mix the water, fresh and dried fruits, sugar, butter, spices, and molasses. Cook on medium-low heat until the mixture begins to boil. Stir occasionally. Lower heat and cook another 10 minutes. Let mixture cool. For convenience, this can sit covered and chilled, several hours or overnight.

Preheat oven to 350°F and grease all pans.

Add the liqueur, extracts, beaten eggs, flour, baking soda, and salt. Mix well. Add nuts, if using.

Fill loaf or ring pans two-thirds of the way up and bake for 30 minutes, then turn down heat to 325°F and bake another 15 to 30 minutes, depending on size, until the tops are a deep brown and feel firm to the touch.

Cool for 20 minutes. While still warm, remove from pans and drizzle with more liqueur. Cool before wrapping and storing. These should be left in a cool place for at least one month. Drizzle with liqueur once more before selling.

For variations of this recipe see the file on the CD:

Cakes

Yield: 4-5 medium loaves

2 cups water

3 cups mixed light and dark raisins

1/2 cup chopped dates

3/4 cup dried apricots, chopped

4 medium apples, chopped

2 cups sugar

1/2 cup butter

1 tablespoon cinnamon

1 teaspoon nutmeg

2 tablespoons molasses

1/2 cup Grand Marnier, plus more for drizzling atop baked loaves

2 teaspoons vanilla extract

2 teaspoons orange extract

2 large eggs, beaten

4 cups unbleached flour

1 scant tablespoon baking soda

1 teaspoon salt

Optional: 2 cups chopped nuts

Chapter 14
Expanding Your Business

Contrary to standard business practice, growing a business is not always the next logical step. It's important to feel comfortable with your business and not let others' ideas of what is best push you along. If you're basically happy with your business — how much income you generate, the type of products you make, the ease in which your life and work schedule flow — then continue with what you are doing. If you're unhappy about a few things, focus on changing those particular issues. This would be a good opportunity to re-evaluate and revise your business plan.

If you want to make changes because you're interested in making more money, you will need to first think about growth. There's a difference between growing your business by increasing your income and moving out of your kitchen and into a storefront.

1. Keeping Your Business at Home

Suppose your business is going well and you're making money, but you want to earn more money. One option is to work within the confines of your kitchen while expanding your production capability, product line, and/or increasing your outlcts.

If you haven't already set up your business end, it's now time to do this. Go back to Chapter 4 and read about becoming a formal, legal, responsible business and do whatever you haven't already done in terms of having a legitimate business format. This doesn't mean you must hire a lawyer and an accountant, and open a business bank account. It means that you've already survived the first scary steps of going into business, which is baking and selling, and now you must fill in the blanks. The blanks may include calling the health department for a license or setting up a ledger or filing a tax return for your business income. If you want to grow your business, at some point you must take these steps to get there. It can be tedious and annoying, but you'll feel better when you can stop worrying that someone might turn you in.

The following sections will help you to increase output and business income.

1.1 Increase production capability

Review your work schedule and see where you can become more efficient in production. Often, a recipe yield can be doubled without doubling your labor, by simply adding on a little extra time; or you can improve efficiency by making dry mixes and/or batters and dough to refrigerate or freeze for later use. (See Chapter 11 to review the details.)

1.2 Upgrade equipment

Decide where you need to make equipment changes in order to increase production. A second oven or a commercial-sized oven that holds a couple of full sheet pans can make a huge difference to your output. You'll probably also need to increase or reorganize your storage area, and perhaps buy a freezer or a larger mixer.

1.3 Renovation

If you've been doing your business for a while and have a steady income, but your production capability is pushed to the limit, decide if modification to the kitchen work area will give you enough extra space. If you have a basement or garage, renovation may give you the capability to increase production. Another option is to build a work area or addition to the house. These suggestions would still be less costly than renting a retail space.

1.4 Increase your outlets

Find new customers by looking in both the retail and wholesale sectors. If something is holding you back from expanding your sales (e.g., lack of proper labels or setting up a delivery route), find solutions to these issues. (Review Chapter 9 on finding customers.)

1.5 Extend your product varieties

Line extensions are new products that are basically the same as your existing products, but with minor changes. By tweaking the flavor, form, shape, or by adding a filling or changing a name, a new product can be marketed without having to make many changes in your operation.

Additionally, your products can be turned into a line of gift items and sold to corporate accounts, through retail outlets, and advertised directly to the public.

1.6 Profit from emerging trends

Fads and trends cycle through our culture. When things are popular, sales thrive. Read the food magazines, watch for new products launched through trade groups, keep an eye on retail bakeries, watch what people are eating, and add trendy foods to your product line.

1.7 Continue to advertise

If you haven't already been using an advertising campaign, now may be the time to start. Advertising takes many forms, not just placing an ad with your local media. Create flyers announcing new products or calling attention to your specialty; send out brochures to area businesses; design a website with contact information; or donate goods to community projects.

Remember, it's often easier to sell more items to an already existing customer than it is to find new customers, so try inserting coupons with your best-selling products or use point-of-sale merchandising to draw attention to any products that sit on a shelf. Add on to your product list; for example, if you sell muffins and coffee cakes through a deli, maybe those customers would also buy desserts to take home. Review Chapter 10 for more promotional and advertising advice.

2. Opening a Retail Shop

If you've got the right mix of ambition, personality, and common sense, opening a retail business can be an exciting adventure. However, statistics say that 50 percent of all businesses fail in the first five years, and that figure increases significantly for food businesses. This means that many ventures don't succeed.

No one starts out thinking "I want to fail," but it happens more than half the time. The reasons for business failure can include:

- Not enough starting or working capital

- Poor management skills

- Unrealistic market expectations

I recently met a woman who was excited about opening a gluten-free bakery and café. She claimed to have a business degree but had no baking or retail experience. She was excited and confident that her concept would work. The business closed within a month. What went wrong? I don't know the internal details, but she was doomed from the beginning. Her small-town bakery sold a very limited product line from a renovated old house situated on a side street in a neglected, low-income, residential neighborhood.

If you are determined, be smart about how you proceed. If you've been working from your home kitchen, then you're already selling products, have a customer base, and, most importantly, have made a reasonable assessment of market needs. As you move ahead, you should certainly be excited, but use rational judgment instead of blind enthusiasm.

Opening a storefront can be an exciting time, but understand that running a retail bakery can be a challenge. Make sure you're familiar with the alternatives before moving ahead. You don't want to find that after you've moved into a retail shop with all the headaches of start-up capital, fixed overhead, employees, and daily shop hours that you look back at your home-based beginning as "the good old days."

You may feel it's important to take the next step and open a retail business. If this is your direction, I have two major suggestions:

- Create a comprehensive business plan so you can manage your growth.

- Before opening a shop, work in an environment close to the kind you expect to operate. The experience will be invaluable.

Once you start making plans for a retail store, life will be different. You'll need financing, legal advice, bookkeeping help, and (unless you already have a location in mind) a good real estate rental agent.

To get your new location approved, city and state or province requirements must be addressed. If you will be renting a storefront, there are landlord and lease issues along with the build-out to get your shop up to code. Even if you're renting property, there still may be costs for renovation to accommodate your business needs.

If you want to buy a building, there are a myriad of other details to be worked out. I do consulting work in this area and when I list the issues, clients are surprised at the extensive to-do list even before the shop opens. The steps you take to own a commercial building are the same as when you purchase a home (i.e., making an offer, procuring a mortgage). You will have to comply with stringent building codes, you'll need expert legal and financial advice, and the services of an architect or drafting professional are necessary to create your floor plan and construction documents.

Zoning needs to be researched before you buy. The building should already be in a commercially zoned area, but the zoning or building code requirements may have changed. A change in ownership means that you must comply with all the current regulations.

There are many other things to consider: Is the plumbing and electricity up to code? Do you have enough reserve capital for repairs if the roof leaks or the air conditioner needs replacing? Will the most logical place for your oven (in terms of production needs) work with your ventilation?

Buying commercial property is a serious commitment requiring a sizeable down payment. This may reduce the amount of capital available for your business growth. But didn't you want to buy the building to grow your business? Buying commercial property might be a good investment, but it's important to research every angle to minimize problems later.

Once you open for business in a retail location, your life will change. Posted hours mean that you'd better be open when you say you will be or you'll lose customers. You'll need display cases full of fresh products and employees to help with the production and sales.

When you own a retail business outside the home, you will encounter many salespeople who want to sell you their products for your business. You need to be skeptical of shysters and hucksters, salespeople and consultants, and people who make a living by selling you *their* ideas and products. Maybe you do need a new convection oven, but first learn what the darn thing is, the pros and cons, and how it affects your floor plan and permits. Perhaps

you do need one; but not the salesperson's new convection oven when a used one can be purchased somewhere else. Be familiar with your products and projected business line — only you will know if a new fryer fits into your plan for making health foods, or if a soft-serve ice cream machine (which must be cleaned daily) is better than a commercial freezer for hard-pack ice cream. Before making a decision, research everything you don't know and don't be pressured into buying anything.

3. Wholesale Space

If you need a larger workspace and your business is primarily wholesale, a good option can be to find an affordable space in a commercial area, away from the higher-rent main route. The move will require rent, utilities, business insurance, additional equipment, and employees. Remember that increased volume will need to pay for the large increase in overhead.

You'll need to rethink the entire production process, from start to finish. Food ventures or small-business development centers can help. When you're interested in scaling up production for a wider distribution, there are many kinks to work out such as shelf life, packaging, and labels. The biggest single product issue is that a change in production method results in a changed product, since ingredients react differently when handled in different ways.

The upside to a wholesale space is your ability to dramatically increase production by bringing in commercial equipment. At this point you should consider focusing on a product, or line of products, that already show potential, and work on their further distribution. It's a big step, but can be worth pursuing. If you're interested in marketing your products as *gourmet* or *specialty*, contact the National

Association for the Specialty Food Trade, Inc. (NASFT).

4. Co-Packers

If you sell a product line that does not vary (e.g., pound packages of granola or biscotti), an alternative to finding a location for your wholesale production is to find a co-packer, a company you contract to manufacture and package your product. These companies either manufacture their own products (and have extra capacity to help another business) or their sole business is to produce others' goods. These businesses often offer services such as product development and distribution. (There is a list of co-packer companies included in the Resources file on the CD.)

5. Making Decisions

You don't have to make all of these decisions immediately. Think about options, reread this book, talk with family and friends, take an open-minded look at your intended market-place, and make a list of reflective questions. Only you know what's best for you. The decision to make a change does not have to come immediately; it can wait until you're sure about what you want.

Thank you for letting me help and my best to everyone. I wish good fortune for all of you. Please visit me at www.bakingfix.com.